Llewellyn's 1995 Magical Almanac

D.J. Conway
Edain McCoy
Silver RavenWolf
&
Patricia Telesco

Contributors:
Susan Baxter
Mary Brown
Paul Harrington
MaraKay Rogers
&
Eirene Varley

Editor/Designer: Cynthia Ahlquist
Cover Design: Christopher Wells

Calendar Section Contributors:
Research/Format: Roxanna Rejali
Design: Robin Wood

Original drawings by Anne Marie Garrison. Clip art from Dover Publications.

Special thanks to Amber Wolfe for the use of daily color and stone correspondences. For more detailed information, please see *Personal Alchemy* by Amber Wolfe, published by Llewellyn Publications.

ISBN 1-56718-906-7

Llewellyn Publications
A Division of Llewellyn Worldwide, Ltd.
P.O. Box 64383-906
St. Paul, MN 55164-0383

EDITOR'S NOTE: It was truly a pleasure compiling *Llewellyn's 1995 Magical Almanac* and working with the authors. D.J. Conway, Edain McCoy, Silver RavenWolf, and Patricia Telesco lend four distinct voices from the magical community to the *Almanac*'s pages; each with its own charm and wisdom. All are accomplished authors, and Llewellyn Publications is proud to be their publisher.

D.J. CONWAY has been involved in many aspects of New Age religion, from the teaching of Yogananda to the study of Qabala, healing herbs, and Wicca. Although she is an ordained minister in two New Age churches and holder of a Doctor of Divinity degree, Conway claims that her heart lies within the Pagan cultures. No longer actively lecturing, Conway has centered her energies on writing. Her published works include *Celtic Magic, Norse Magic, Ancient and Shining Ones* and the upcoming *Maid, Mother, Crone; Dancing With Dragons; By Oak, Ash and Thorn; Moon Magick; Flying Without a Broom;* and *Animal Magick.*

EDAIN MCCOY is currently pursuing a graduate degree in Cultural History at Indiana

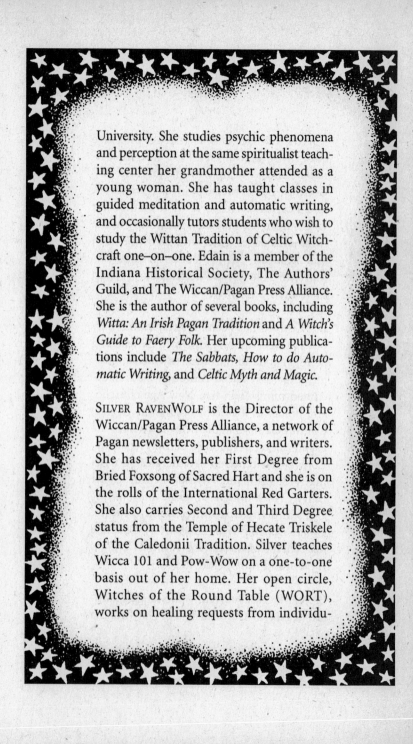

University. She studies psychic phenomena and perception at the same spiritualist teaching center her grandmother attended as a young woman. She has taught classes in guided meditation and automatic writing, and occasionally tutors students who wish to study the Wittan Tradition of Celtic Witchcraft one–on–one. Edain is a member of the Indiana Historical Society, The Authors' Guild, and The Wiccan/Pagan Press Alliance. She is the author of several books, including *Witta: An Irish Pagan Tradition* and *A Witch's Guide to Faery Folk.* Her upcoming publications include *The Sabbats, How to do Automatic Writing,* and *Celtic Myth and Magic.*

SILVER RAVENWOLF is the Director of the Wiccan/Pagan Press Alliance, a network of Pagan newsletters, publishers, and writers. She has received her First Degree from Bried Foxsong of Sacred Hart and she is on the rolls of the International Red Garters. She also carries Second and Third Degree status from the Temple of Hecate Triskele of the Caledonii Tradition. Silver teaches Wicca 101 and Pow-Wow on a one-to-one basis out of her home. Her open circle, Witches of the Round Table (WORT), works on healing requests from individu-

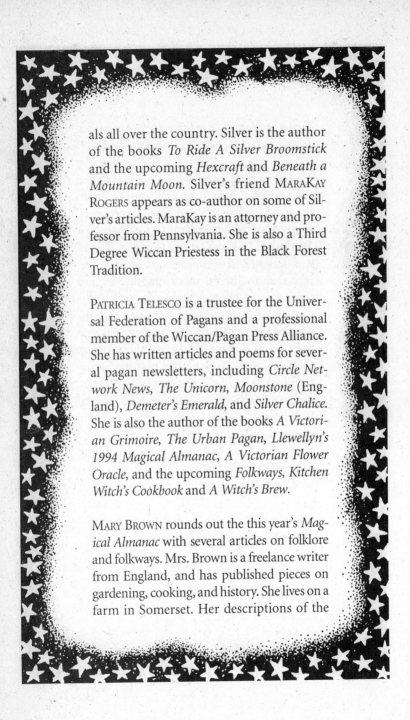

als all over the country. Silver is the author of the books *To Ride A Silver Broomstick* and the upcoming *Hexcraft* and *Beneath a Mountain Moon*. Silver's friend MARAKAY ROGERS appears as co-author on some of Silver's articles. MaraKay is an attorney and professor from Pennsylvania. She is also a Third Degree Wiccan Priestess in the Black Forest Tradition.

PATRICIA TELESCO is a trustee for the Universal Federation of Pagans and a professional member of the Wiccan/Pagan Press Alliance. She has written articles and poems for several pagan newsletters, including *Circle Network News*, *The Unicorn*, *Moonstone* (England), *Demeter's Emerald*, and *Silver Chalice*. She is also the author of the books *A Victorian Grimoire*, *The Urban Pagan*, *Llewellyn's 1994 Magical Almanac*, *A Victorian Flower Oracle*, and the upcoming *Folkways*, *Kitchen Witch's Cookbook* and *A Witch's Brew*.

MARY BROWN rounds out the this year's *Magical Almanac* with several articles on folklore and folkways. Mrs. Brown is a freelance writer from England, and has published pieces on gardening, cooking, and history. She lives on a farm in Somerset. Her descriptions of the

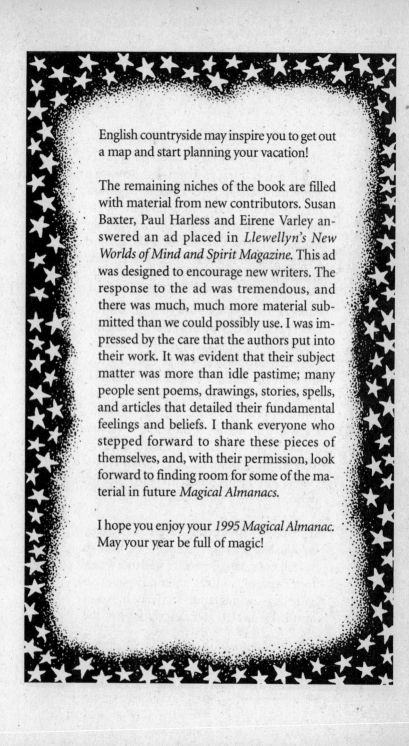

English countryside may inspire you to get out a map and start planning your vacation!

The remaining niches of the book are filled with material from new contributors. Susan Baxter, Paul Harless and Eirene Varley answered an ad placed in *Llewellyn's New Worlds of Mind and Spirit Magazine.* This ad was designed to encourage new writers. The response to the ad was tremendous, and there was much, much more material submitted than we could possibly use. I was impressed by the care that the authors put into their work. It was evident that their subject matter was more than idle pastime; many people sent poems, drawings, stories, spells, and articles that detailed their fundamental feelings and beliefs. I thank everyone who stepped forward to share these pieces of themselves, and, with their permission, look forward to finding room for some of the material in future *Magical Almanacs.*

I hope you enjoy your *1995 Magical Almanac.* May your year be full of magic!

Table of Contents

Superstitions Throughout the Year 1

A Prosperity Charm for the New Year............................. 8

Affirmations: Not Just A New Age Joke.......................... 9

The Mystical Timepiece 12

What Day Is It? 14

January 6: The Epiphany of Kore 18

Standard Magickal First Aid 19

February 4: The Festival of King Frost 23

When Jack Frost Bites : Try These Family Cold Remedies....... 24

Natural Remedies for Wintertime Ailments 26

When Your Child is Ill: The Sympathy Doll..................... 30

The Simple Beauty of Candle Magic.............................. 33

The Muses 34

Just a Touch of Love 36

Valentine's Day Divinations 38

The Romantic Allure of Magical Scent........................... 40

The Magic of Mardi Gras 42

March 15: The Festival of Anna Perenna........................ 47

Babe on a Broomstick: Aspecting Your Beauty Within.......... 48

Crystal Gazing and Scrying.. 52

Discovering Dragons 54

The Beginning.. 58

Protecting and Purifying Potpourris for Spring Cleaning....... 59

The Lore of Canis Familiaris...................................... 62

Handling the Magickal Emergency 64

Lady Day: An Ancient Festival 66

The Pagan Past of Ireland's Oldest Symbol 68

How the Gods Stole Back the Spring *An Anglo Saxon Myth* 70

April Fool's Day: The Lord of Misrule Rides Again 72

Calling in Minerva: Three Witches Experience Aspecting 73

Strange Animal Superstitions 76

The Minor Magicks 79

Mantra on Music 83

A Cup of Unity 84

A Lusty Brew for Beltaine 85

May 9, 11, and 13: The Ancient Festival of Lumeria 86

Faery Sweet Breads 87

Flowers, Herbs, and the Faeries of May 88

Oils for Attuning with the Elements 93

From the Scent Shop 96

The Birthday Rattle 98

June 15: A Feast of Vestalia 99

Wishing Trees 100

The New Year of the Trees 101

Tree Folklore 104

The Snake and the Hunter: A Teaching Game 108

Animal Weather Omens 110

Introduction to the Almanac 111

Time Changes 114

1995 Sabbats and Full Moons 115

January 116

February 121

March 125

April 130

May 135

June 140

July 145

August. 150

September 155

October 160

November 165

December 170

June 25: The Feast of the Hunter's Moon 175

Excuse Me, This Magickal Thingie Doesn't Work 176

Practical Magick in a Pinch. 178

Romantic Rosemary. 179

The Magic of Garlic 184

July 7: Tanabata, A Day for Lovers 187

Have Magick, Will Travel: The Marvelous Medicine Bag 188

Tibetan Divination 194

The Magic of Wells and Springs 197

July 23: Neptunalia 200

The Witches' Bottle. 202

August 1: The Festival of Green Corn 205

Harvest Home. 206

August 22: Tij, A Holiday for Women 210

Magical Apple Lore. 211

Tea To'tlers' Wine. 215

What Do You Mean, Your Spells Don't Work?. 216

Hair Superstitions 220

Wells: A Deep Subject 222

September 19: The Festival of Chang-O 223

Attuning Your Home with Dragon Energy 224

Fun Things with the Tarot. 229

October 31: Lating Night 232

Who's Afraid of the Big Bad Crone? 234

Incenses to Assist in Conjuring Spirits 238

Unleashing the Magic in Your Fireplace 240

Don't Have a Fireplace? Build a Hearth! 242

Fires and Feasting 243

November 18: The Feast of Baba Yaga 247

Honegar: A European Magical Tonic 248

A Boiling Potpourri for the Magical Kitchen 250

Holiday Baking Tips 251

December 17-23: Saturnalia 254

Give the Gift of Magick 255

Fateful Stones: A Brief Look at Mysterious Gems 261

And to You Your Wassail, too! 262

The Yule Wish Tree 264

The Twelve Days of Christmas 265

Directory of Products and Services 269

Superstitions Throughout the Year

By D.J. Conway

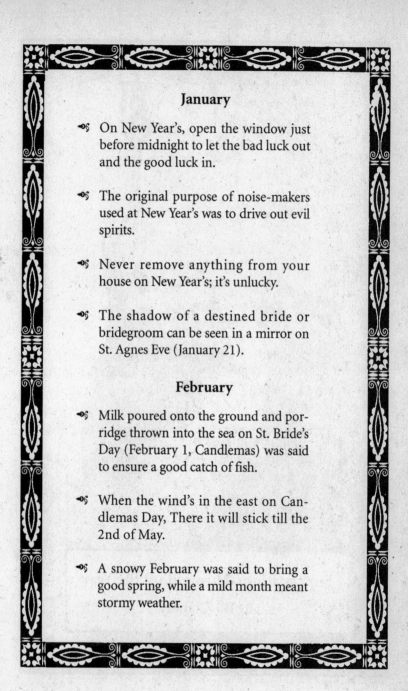

January

-⧽ On New Year's, open the window just before midnight to let the bad luck out and the good luck in.

-⧽ The original purpose of noise-makers used at New Year's was to drive out evil spirits.

-⧽ Never remove anything from your house on New Year's; it's unlucky.

-⧽ The shadow of a destined bride or bridegroom can be seen in a mirror on St. Agnes Eve (January 21).

February

-⧽ Milk poured onto the ground and porridge thrown into the sea on St. Bride's Day (February 1, Candlemas) was said to ensure a good catch of fish.

-⧽ When the wind's in the east on Candlemas Day, There it will stick till the 2nd of May.

-⧽ A snowy February was said to bring a good spring, while a mild month meant stormy weather.

◦§ Any enterprise begun on February 29 is sure of success.

March

◦§ In Devonshire, England, the last 3 days in March were called the Blind Days. It was unlucky to sow any seed during that time.

◦§ If you find the first daffodil of the spring, you will have more gold than silver that year.

◦§ Windows of a house should be kept shut on March 1st to prevent fleas entering. Then the house will be free of fleas for the rest of the year.

◦§ Drink nettle tea in March, and mugwort tea in May; and cowslip wine in June, to send decline away.

April

◦§ The Sun dances at its rising on Easter Sunday morning.

◦§ Bread baked on Good Friday will not go moldy.

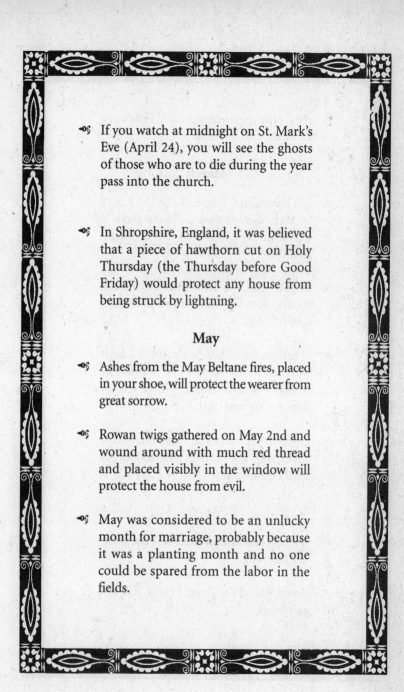

◦§ If you watch at midnight on St. Mark's Eve (April 24), you will see the ghosts of those who are to die during the year pass into the church.

◦§ In Shropshire, England, it was believed that a piece of hawthorn cut on Holy Thursday (the Thursday before Good Friday) would protect any house from being struck by lightning.

May

◦§ Ashes from the May Beltane fires, placed in your shoe, will protect the wearer from great sorrow.

◦§ Rowan twigs gathered on May 2nd and wound around with much red thread and placed visibly in the window will protect the house from evil.

◦§ May was considered to be an unlucky month for marriage, probably because it was a planting month and no one could be spared from the labor in the fields.

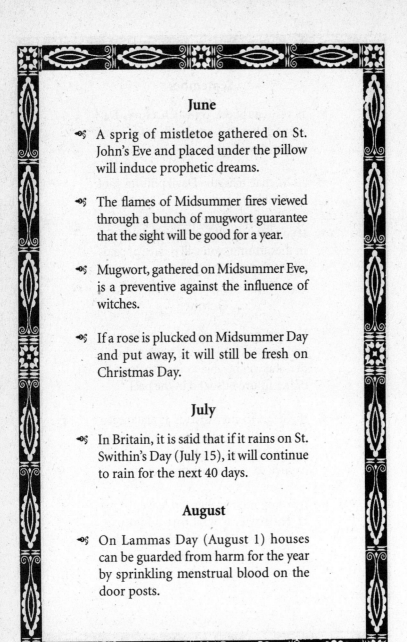

June

- A sprig of mistletoe gathered on St. John's Eve and placed under the pillow will induce prophetic dreams.

- The flames of Midsummer fires viewed through a bunch of mugwort guarantee that the sight will be good for a year.

- Mugwort, gathered on Midsummer Eve, is a preventive against the influence of witches.

- If a rose is plucked on Midsummer Day and put away, it will still be fresh on Christmas Day.

July

- In Britain, it is said that if it rains on St. Swithin's Day (July 15), it will continue to rain for the next 40 days.

August

- On Lammas Day (August 1) houses can be guarded from harm for the year by sprinkling menstrual blood on the door posts.

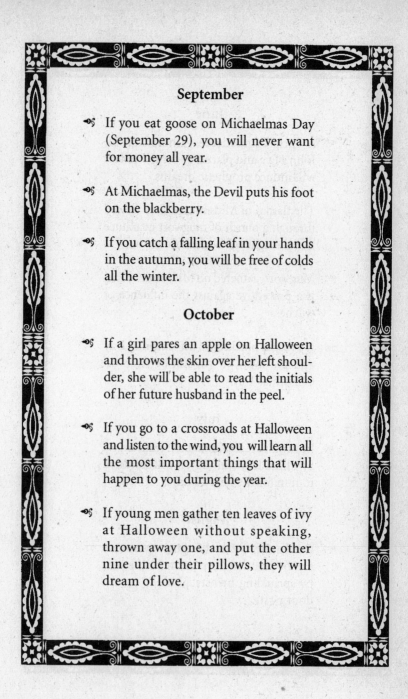

September

❧ If you eat goose on Michaelmas Day (September 29), you will never want for money all year.

❧ At Michaelmas, the Devil puts his foot on the blackberry.

❧ If you catch a falling leaf in your hands in the autumn, you will be free of colds all the winter.

October

❧ If a girl pares an apple on Halloween and throws the skin over her left shoulder, she will be able to read the initials of her future husband in the peel.

❧ If you go to a crossroads at Halloween and listen to the wind, you will learn all the most important things that will happen to you during the year.

❧ If young men gather ten leaves of ivy at Halloween without speaking, thrown away one, and put the other nine under their pillows, they will dream of love.

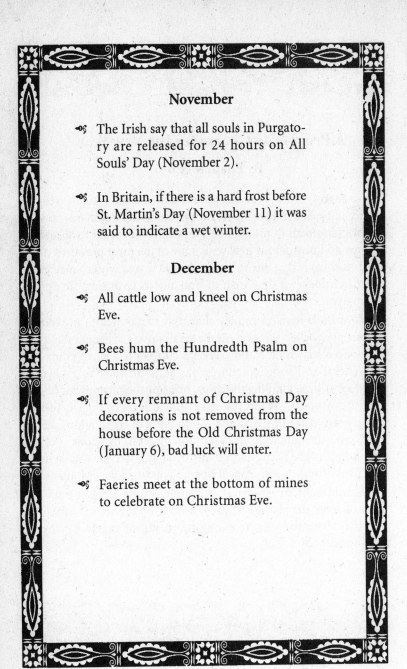

November

- The Irish say that all souls in Purgatory are released for 24 hours on All Souls' Day (November 2).

- In Britain, if there is a hard frost before St. Martin's Day (November 11) it was said to indicate a wet winter.

December

- All cattle low and kneel on Christmas Eve.

- Bees hum the Hundredth Psalm on Christmas Eve.

- If every remnant of Christmas Day decorations is not removed from the house before the Old Christmas Day (January 6), bad luck will enter.

- Faeries meet at the bottom of mines to celebrate on Christmas Eve.

A Prosperity Charm for the New Year

By Edain McCoy

The changing of the year has always been a time fraught with magic, and every culture has its superstitions and lore about how this brief moment in time should be observed in order to ensure a happy and prosperous new year. One of the most prevalent of these customs is that one must start the new year with money in his or her pocket if they wish to find any there during the upcoming year.

To make a magical money charm to attract wealth to your own empty pockets you will need a small square of green or gold cloth and a matching ribbon, several coins, a few small cinnamon sticks, and some patchouly oil. Early on New Year's Eve spend some time fondling the coins, infusing them with your desire for prosperity. When you have done this for as long as you can, place a drop of patchouly oil on each of them and place them, with the cinnamon sticks, in the center of the cloth. Pull up the ends of the fabric and tie the top shut. Place the charm in your pocket or purse which will be with you when the year turns.

At midnight, or whenever else you (or your magical tradition) observe the change of time, hold it tight and remember that it is there for you, releasing its wealth of magic for the coming year.

Affirm ①

Affirmations: Not Just a New Age Joke

By Silver RavenWolf

The simplicity of affirmations fools you. Many people feel that anything so effortless cannot be useful. An affirmation is the process of stating a positive goal as if it has already happened. Patterned around positive ideas, it allows the mind to focus on a singular thought form. Designed to align our energies with those of the universe, the thought form then accomplishes our goal. There are a few rules:

The statement must be in the present tense. With affirmations, your world is the here and now — the present. If you say, "I will become a wise person," you are defeating the purpose of the statement. Rather, you should say, "I am a wise person." Begin with words like: I am, It is, I embrace, I welcome, I enjoy, I understand.

The statement should revolve around a positive thought. Never say, "I move out of poverty." Poverty is a negative word and implies something you don't have. Another no-no would be, "I am not sick anymore." The word sick also has negative implications. Stick to positive, upbeat ideas. "I am full of healthy energy."

The statement should be short and to-the-point. "I greet the day with sunshine in my heart, love surrounding my body, wisdom in my soul and all my needs met," is a little overdoing it. Choose simple statements with powerful thrusts. When you speak, you are pushing the thought vibrations into the universe.

Finally, the statement should conform to your belief structure. If you live in a no-limit world already, affirmations will not be difficult for you, but if you are a person who knows your limitations, then you will need to compose statements that conform with your self-imposed boundaries.

There are two types of affirmations: Those composed to reach a specific goal, and those manufactured by constant, internal dialogue to counteract negative thinking.

Let's spend a moment with the quickie affirmations. Listen to yourself think. We all talk to ourselves, especially when we are doing something boring. If these thoughts are negative in nature, it will have an effect on our performance, both short and long-term.

Written and recorded affirmations for your listening convenience work well. The third type, affirmations done during meditation, lend themselves well to magickal applications. Of the

three, affirmations done while you are in the alpha state are more likely to take effect faster than the other two procedures, however, all three methods will carry the same long-term effects.

The only major glitch in using affirmations resides with the human desire to have events take shape immediately. Too often I have seen people begin a program of affirmations and give up after a week or two because they are not seeing the benefits fast enough. For affirmations to be beneficial, you must work with them for at least thirty days, no breaks.

There is a debate on the optimum timing for using affirmations. Many psychologists believe that their performance should coincide with your first thought in the morning. I don't know about you, but mornings and I are not compatible. I am also lousy at following a pattern or schedule. To outsmart myself, I do my affirmations during meditation at the end of the day when I am too pooped to run off and do something else.

Affirmations are not a new age joke. They are building blocks in our desire to create positive self-esteem for ourselves, which in turn affects those about us. Affirmations do work, in a domino effect. If I am in a good mood, I create a good environment that enhances the lives of my children, my spouse, and my friends.

The Mystical Timepiece

By Patricia Telesco

✗ Midnight is considered the witching hour because it hangs in the balance between night and day. This is the time when the spirits of the dead are closest to the realms of the living.

✗ The word clock comes from the Latin term "clocca," meaning bell.

✗ For good luck, one should wind clocks fully after the toll of midnight on New Year's Eve.

✗ The tripod seat at the Oracle of Delphi is considered by historians to be symbolic of the past, present, and future.

✗ The Greek God, Kronos, is the father of time. He is thought to live backwards in time, having died before he was born. The Roman equivalent is Saturn.

✠ The sundial was fashioned after the solar disk. The first accurate sundial appeared in China around 1 AD, and was divided into 100 units.

✠ A clock facing the fire will cause the flame to go out. This belief has its roots in the old idea that fire was stolen from the sun, so any representation of the sun will not allow it to burn fully.

✠ In rural England it is often the custom to stop a clock at the time of a person's death and not start it again until the body is removed from the house.

✠ Some churches in Europe stop the chiming of the hours during hymns, believing that if the clock should strike twelve while the songs are sung, a parishioner will pass over by the next Sunday.

✠ If a clock chimes just before a bride enters the church it is a very fortunate sign for the marriage.

✠ If a clock strikes the wrong hour it portends ill fortune to come in the number of hours indicated by the chimes.

What Day Is It?

By D.J. Conway

Sneeze on a Monday, sneeze for danger. Sneeze on a Tuesday, kiss a stranger. Sneeze on a Wednesday, get a letter. Sneeze on a Thursday, something better. Sneeze on a Friday, sneeze for sorrow. Sneeze on Saturday, see your true love tomorrow.

Monday's child is fair of face; Tuesday's child is full of grace; Wednesday's child is full of woe; Thursday's child has far to go; Friday's child is loving and giving; Saturday's child works hard for a living. But the child that is born on the Sabbath Day is blithe and bonny, good and gay.

A New England rhyme about the days of the week goes: Monday for health, Tuesday for wealth, Wednesday the best of all, Thursday for losses, Friday for crosses, And Saturday no luck at all.

Monday

Almost every culture believed that if the New Moon came on Monday (Moon-day), it was a sign of good weather and good luck. In several sections of England it is said that 3 particular Mondays of the year are very unlucky: the first Monday in April, the second Monday in August, and the last Monday in December. As Monday goes, so goes the week.

Tuesday

It is unfortunate to meet a left-handed person on a Tuesday morning, but fortunate to meet one on any other day of the week. This may come from the legend of the Scandinavian god Tyr, or Tiw, whose name is the origin of Tuesday.

Wednesday

Although most Europeans considered Wednesday an unlucky day, those in the U.S.A. considered it very lucky.

Thursday

Thursday has one lucky hour—the hour before the sun rises.

Friday

It is unlucky to start a new job on a Friday.

Many cultures believed that it was unlucky to be born, marry, begin a new job, sail a ship, cut your nails, or move to a new house on a Friday.

Bad luck will attend a ship that sails on a Friday. This idea may have come from the H.M.S. Friday; the construction of this ship was begun on a Friday, it sailed on a Friday, and disappeared without a trace.

In Hungary, the bad luck of being born on a Friday could be circumvented by putting a few drops of your blood on a piece cut from your clothing and then burning it.

The Scots and Germans said Friday was a good day for courting.

Even the criminal element had superstitions about Friday. Any burglary committed on a Friday would not be successful and would lead to arrest. It was bad luck to go to trial on a Friday.

To cut the fingernails on a Friday or a Sunday will bring bad luck.

Saturday

The Irish say that if you see a rainbow on a Saturday, the entire following week will be stormy.

Many European countries believe that the Sun always shines some part of every Saturday.

The Scots say that anyone born on a Saturday can see ghosts.

Moving on a Saturday means a short stay.

If a New Moon falls on a Saturday, there will be 20 days of wind and rain.

Sunday

It is unlucky to turn a feather bed on Sunday.

In Denmark, a child born on a Sunday is said to have the Second Sight.

In Yorkshire, England, a child born on a Sunday was said to be safe from ill-wishing.

Water drawn from downstream before sunrise, and in silence, on any Sunday morning, in one jug from 3 separate and flowing springs, will remain pure for a year, and has healing properties. Wales.

If you sneeze on a Sunday before breakfast, you will be in love forever.

January 6: The Epiphany of Kore

By Edain McCoy

In ancient Alexandria, a drama which was part ritual, part theater, was enacted commemorating Kore's return to the earth from her six months of Underworld exile. Kore is a Goddess of fertility and grains who was particularly beloved by the women of the Mediterranean region. Today she is often evoked for her powers of protection and healing.

KAY WOMRATH

Standard Magickal First Aid

By Silver RavenWolf

Meditation.

Every day, for at least one month, you should work on moving into alpha through meditation.

Banishing.

The Lesser Banishing Pentagram ritual, properly done and with intent behind it, can get rid of almost anything. When in doubt, do this before doing anything else. And I mean anything. It may only be a temporary problem solver, because after all, if you are talking about a haunting, you will need more. It does buy you some time to plan and properly execute a larger magickal application. Like grandma's chicken soup, the Lesser Banishing Ritual can't hurt.

Instant Holy Water.

Nothing is easier than this one. Get a paper cup and a packet of salt (like from a fast food restaurant). Breathe deeply, go into alpha with the three, two, one method. Exorcise the water, say anything. Tell it that it has been exorcised and trace a banishing pentagram over it. Same thing for the salt. Pour the salt in, stir it — you've got fingers — and say something — again, anything; announcing that you're making holy water, works just fine.

Amulets.

Grasp the amulet-to-be firmly in hand. Breathe; draw down or aspect. Make some spiffy banishing gestures over it with your free hand and exorcise the thing, then tell it what it is being charged to do, and why. Call on your favorite elemental kings or archangels; do the Witches' Rune; make some appropriate invoking gestures over it with your free hand. Again, intent, intent, intent. If you are doing it in a kitchen or at a restaurant, make holy water to sprinkle on it . If you have a lighter in your pocket, use the element of fire.

Exorcising and Breaking Hexes.

Make holy water, fast. Splash it all over the thing — ring, bracelet, whatever; if it is paper, sprinkle lightly or just use salt. Do more of the spiffy banishing gestures and a banishing pentagram while you are at it. Use more holy water. If it is waterproof, dunk the thing right in the glass. Good for removing spells on just about anything, as long as they're not too strong (and most aren't). If you are worried, breathe and draw down or aspect, then cast a circle in your head if you must, as quickly as you can; do all of the banishing right in the circle.

Help! There's a THING in the House!

First, make sure you are not being fooled. Then, make sure you are not being confronted by the Son of the Amityville Horror.

This is not going to be quick or easy first aid; it takes an hour to an hour and a half minimum to clear out the average seven-or-eight room house. For non-manifesting problems, meaning there is nothing floating around, you must go through with holy water, incense, candle and bell, as well as banishing in every single room before and after. Then all the doors and windows must be sealed. Every room must "feel" cleared out. Ask the residents of the house or apartment if the place feels better. If it does not, repeat the procedure and allow them to watch you this time. If this general procedure does not clear the place out — admit defeat, and call an expert. If something is too complicated, be willing to admit it; don't risk danger to yourself to pull off something beyond your own ability.

Ooops, I Forgot my Spell!

Keep on going. Of course, if you do this all the time, there is no excuse for not knowing your material. But, should you truly forget, consider the end result and just ask for that. Get the intent visualized. Can't remember how to banish? There is actually a person on this earth who has such sufficient force that they can banish by pointing at the object, dancing around like a banshee, and calling out, "Eenie meanie miney moe, all bad juju's gotta go!" It-uh-works. Ahem.

Ah, It Won't Go Away...

Read Lovecraft — don't call up anything you can't send back. If someone else pulls this stunt (you won't because you know to check how to get rid of things first, don't you...), banish like crazy, throw holy water at it, and call loudly for divine intervention if things get rough. This is not a joke.

If all else fails, get out of there yourself. The thing is probably more interested in going after the idiot that called (or bothered) it, but you really don't want to hang around and find out. Write the great fiction novel about it from the sidelines. There's no excuse except sheer stupidity for people who get into this situation. The best advice is to stay away from people who get themselves into this sort of thing anyway. Stay *far* away.

(Un) Holy Horrors! It's Not on the First Aid List!

At least banishing can't hurt, and you can use it if you can't ground and center any other way, so don't panic. Please remember that these lists are for magickal problems, not physical ones, unless those difficulties stem from magick or were created by magickal misfires. You are better off ducking a punch than banishing at a person trying to hit you; use common sense. Magickal first aid isn't for strictly mundane emergencies, though you can combine it with mundane treatment. Call 911 if your house is robbed; then banish to protect it from further negativity and aid the owner's peace of mind. Then you can do a spell to bring the robber to justice.

February 4: The Festival of King Frost

By Edain McCoy

Every February 4th from 1813 until the outbreak of the first World War, Londoners held a festival on the ice of the frozen River Thames in honor of King Frost, a barely concealed version of the Pagan faery king, Jack Frost. Though the nineteenth century celebration was created largely to overcome winter's boredom, no doubt some primal memory of English ancestors making pleas to the Old Gods for spring's quick arrival crept into the observance.

When Jack Frost Bites: Try These Family Cold Remedies

By Silver RavenWolf

When illness strikes, it is an immediate signal to the magickal person that everyday priorities need better scheduling to suit our health and safety. When you get sick, tell the gang to take a number, you've got to take care of yourself. In the meantime, try these remedies that work well for our family.

Simple Cold

1 ounce of tomato juice (or V-8)
1/4 ounce of black pepper
1/8 ounce of cayenne pepper

Mix together in a small glass and drink. (Do it fast.) Repeat three times a day. Works best if you begin as soon as you feel the symptoms coming on.

Flu and Chest Cold Buster

1 ounce of dried Yarrow Flowers
1 pinch of cherry bark
1 mint tea bag (or dried mint)
One cup of water

Boil water in a small pot. Place yarrow flowers and mint tea bag in coffee filter and set gently on top of hot water. Steep for five minutes. Remove filter and discard. Sweeten with honey. Tastes awful, but makes you feel fantastic within 45 minutes. Repeat three times during the day. Use this treatment at the onset of your discomfort, but works very well at any time. Can be taken with antibiotics, but check with your physician first.

Fever Blaster

2 ounces of lavender
1 ounce of grated orange peels
1 small, new, empty cloth bag
    (use thin cloth)

Put ingredients in the bag. Rub bag over the pillow you will sleep on, then put the bag around your neck while you sleep.

Cough Smasher

1/2 teaspoon horehound
1/2 teaspoon hyssop
1/2 teaspoon coltsfoot
1/2 teaspoon slippery elm bark
A dash of lemon.

Follow same instructions under flu buster, let steep for fifteen minutes.

Antibiotic Shortage

Only have a few of those antibiotics left and still fussing with the creeping crud? Diane McDonough of Newville, Pennsylvania says: "Empower them. I'm not kidding! I tried it. Hold the remaining medicine in your hands and ask that each pill safely work ten fold in fighting your illness. Worked for me!"

Natural Remedies for Wintertime Ailments

By Edain McCoy

While no natural remedy should replace the advice and care of a qualified doctor, there are numerous medicines to be found in nature which can help see us through the aches, pains, and chills of winter's colds and flus. Of course, the best medicine is always prevention. The herbs bearberry and garlic have proven themselves to be excellent tonics for the immune system when taken regularly, and are particularly good for helping to make you "cold resistant."

Soup To Help Loosen Congestion

This soup packs a spicy punch, but usually does the trick without resorting to drugs. Purists, please note that the basic ingredient is chicken stock which has proven to help treat colds.

16 ounces chicken broth
1 minced red onion
1/8–1/4 teaspoon powdered cayenne pepper
1 teaspoon dried boneset
1 teaspoon dried chamomile
1/4 teaspoon black pepper
1/4 teaspoon garlic powder
1/8 teaspoon sage
salt if desired for taste

Set all ingredients in a large stock pot to gently boil. Serve steaming hot.

Fever Reducing Tea

Many herbs contain anti-inflammatory properties which have been used successfully to help reduce fevers and ease aches and pains. A fever can be a sign of serious illness, and children under 12 or anyone with a fever that persists for more than two days or goes over 104 degrees should be taken to a doctor. This recipe makes about six cups. It can be kept in the refrigerator for up to three days. It reheats as well in the microwave as over the stove.

1 1/2 tablespoons black willow bark
    (omit if you are allergic to aspirin!)
1 1/2 tablespoons black elder (increase to 2 table-
    spoons if you are omitting the willow bark)
1 teaspoon blessed thistle
1/2 tablespoon goldenseal
2 teaspoons echinacea
1/2 tablespoon linden flowers
1 1/2 teaspoons chamomile

Place the ingredients in a cheesecloth or large tea ball. Tie up the cloth or secure the tea ball and place it into 6 1/2 cups of boiled water. Allow it to steep for at least ten minutes. This tea makes no claim to being the best tasting brew ever created, but it works well. You may add sugar, honey, or rice syrup if you wish. Take one cup every four to six hours as needed.

Natural Cough Suppressant

Using the well-known honey and lemon as a base, this thick paste contains the mild narcotic of bugleweed, a similar property to the chemical codeine which is often prescribed to treat severe coughs. Dry coughs can be treated every four hours. Coughs which are bringing up phlegm should be left alone until bedtime because they are beneficial in purging the illness from your body. In a large bowl thoroughly mix:

1 pound honey
1 1/2 cups lemon juice (avoid oil-based substitutes!)
1/2 tablespoon bugleweed
1/2 tablespoon coltsfoot
8 ounces unsweetened cherries, crushed

This will keep in the refrigerator for about a week. Use 2 to 3 tablespoons every four hours as needed.

Anti-Diarrheal Preparation

While it is usually best to let diarrhea run its course so that whatever is making you sick can escape, there are times when we simply must pull ourselves together and get out of the bathroom. The following recipe is high in vitamin C and healthy bacteria, which can put you back on track without the artificial chemicals found in over-the-counter preparations. In a large bowl mix:

1 1/2 cups crushed blackberries
1/2 cup crushed raspberries or black cherries
1/2 cup strained carrots (the baby food variety is perfect!)
1/2 pound acidophilus yogurt
2 sliced bananas
1/8 teaspoon nutmeg
1/4 teaspoon ginger
1/2 cup cooled, cooked rice (optional)

Chill and eat. This preparation is tasty enough that you won't feel like you're taking your medicine. Eat as much as you like, but don't overdo. The unused portion must be covered and refrigerated.

When Your Child is Ill: The Sympathy Doll

By Silver RavenWolf

When your child is ill, the first order of business is to seek the proper medical care. There is no reason, however, that you cannot mix magick and medicine. Here is an inexpensive and delightful idea for any sick child.

Supplies

1/2 yard of new, unbleached muslin
2 square inches of green felt and of pink felt
Iron-on star appliques
1 yard of green lace
1 yard of pink lace *or* blue lace
1 green candle dressed in healing oil and empowered
1 clipping of the child's hair

Timing

When a child is sick, you can't worry too much about timing. Your best course of action is to choose the right planetary hour for healing. The Moon (children) or Mercury (healing) would be good choices.

1. Tear the muslin into one-inch strips. Save one strip and set it aside.

2. Lay the strips out, one on top of the other. An easy way to do this is hold all the strips together at one end and shake them out, then lay them down.

3. Pick the entire bunch up from the middle and fold them over.

4. Take the strip you saved and tie the bundle together approximately three inches from the top. You should now have a replica of a yarn doll.

5. Measure the doll from the neck down. Cut the lace into strips of this length. Repeat until you have cut all the lace.

6. Sew each piece of lace so that it hangs from the neck.

7. Cut three hearts out of the green felt and three hearts out of the pink felt.

8. Sew the hearts on to a few of the skirt strips

9. Sew the star appliques on the remaining skirt strips.

10. Cleanse, consecrate, and empower the doll in a magick circle.

11. Sew a piece of the child's hair into the head of the doll, tucking it in the strips so that it can not be seen.

12. Ask the Goddess Artemis or Grandmother Ana to heal the child and watch over him or her during his or her recovery process.

14. Hang the doll in the child's room, preferably above the bed.

15. When the child is well you have two choices: Thank Deity and save it until the child is ill again, then cleanse, consecrate and re-empower, or remove the magick, dismember the doll, thank the deities and burn everything.

The Simple Beauty of Candle Magic

By Edain McCoy

Fire has been sacred in every culture on the planet. It was our first source of reliable warmth, a fuel with which to cook, and a comforting light in the dark of night. It is the element of fundamental transformation. Objects caressed by fire are never the same again. Some are destroyed by it, others emerge stronger. Most of the oldest Pagan festivals still known to us honor fire.

Candle magic is intimately linked to the element of fire, and has remained very popular throughout history because of its ease and its effectiveness. The candles can be used as they are, or they can be anointed with special oils in harmony with the magical goal. Potent symbols, such as runes, can also be carved into their sides.

To unleash the magic of the candle, choose one of a color appropriate to your goal, mentally infuse it with your need, then light the candle while remaining focused on your goal. Spend some time meditating on the flame as it burns. If the idea is to banish something from your life, visualize it being consumed. Likewise, if you wish to draw something into your life, see the candle as being the essence of those wishes, and its disappearance as representing your desires being taken into the unseen world where they will gather strength to manifest. Always allow yourself to feel connected to the flame, to know that it embodies your desire.

The Muses

By Eirene Varley

Have you ever felt particularly uninspired and told someone you were "waiting for the Muse to strike?" Well, while you're waiting, here's something for you to muse over.

There are nine Muses in Ancient Greek tradition. They are the daughters of Zeus, King of the Gods, and Mnemosyne, Goddess of Memory.

When the Muses perform for the gods, they are often led by Apollo. The most famous horse in the world, Pegasus, belongs to them.

The Muses have prophetic powers, which they might be willing to share, and they like to teach. Take care not to challenge them to a contest — they are known to mutilate those who dare to draw comparisons. They took away Thamyris's sight and voice, turned the Pierides into birds, and stole the Sirens' wings. The Muses appreciate a sacrifice of milk, honey, or just plain water. Their names are:

- ✥ Calliope "she of the beautiful voice," philosophy, epics. Portrayed with a tablet and stylus; sometimes a scroll.

- ✥ Clio "she who praises," history. Portrayed with books or a scroll.

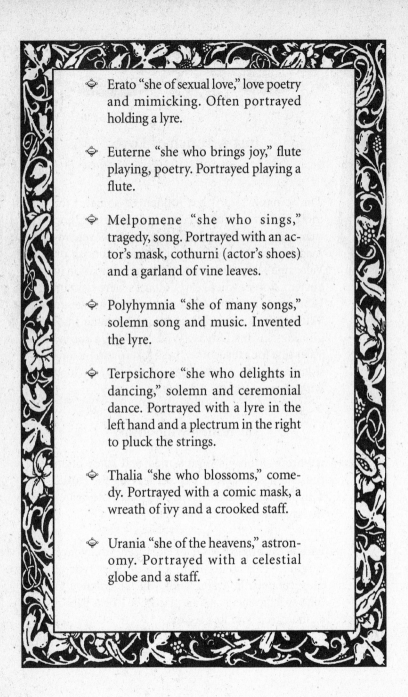

❧ Erato "she of sexual love," love poetry and mimicking. Often portrayed holding a lyre.

❧ Euterne "she who brings joy," flute playing, poetry. Portrayed playing a flute.

❧ Melpomene "she who sings," tragedy, song. Portrayed with an actor's mask, cothurni (actor's shoes) and a garland of vine leaves.

❧ Polyhymnia "she of many songs," solemn song and music. Invented the lyre.

❧ Terpsichore "she who delights in dancing," solemn and ceremonial dance. Portrayed with a lyre in the left hand and a plectrum in the right to pluck the strings.

❧ Thalia "she who blossoms," comedy. Portrayed with a comic mask, a wreath of ivy and a crooked staff.

❧ Urania "she of the heavens," astronomy. Portrayed with a celestial globe and a staff.

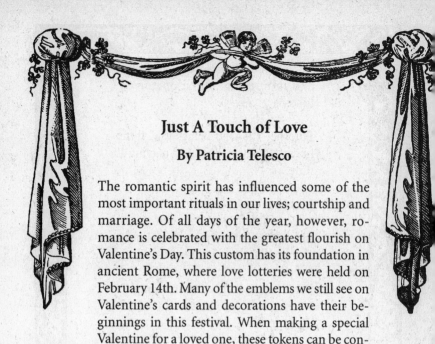

Just A Touch of Love

By Patricia Telesco

The romantic spirit has influenced some of the most important rituals in our lives; courtship and marriage. Of all days of the year, however, romance is celebrated with the greatest flourish on Valentine's Day. This custom has its foundation in ancient Rome, where love lotteries were held on February 14th. Many of the emblems we still see on Valentine's cards and decorations have their beginnings in this festival. When making a special Valentine for a loved one, these tokens can be considered for the special energies they carry along with your messages.

Valentine's Symbolism:

Ribbon—Ribbons were a medieval favor often presented to a knight or lord leaving for battle. This little gift was believed to protect the bearer through the power of devotion.

Lace—The original word for lace meant "to snare or capture." This comes from a much older type of magic popular in Arabic lands, which used knots to bind specific energy in one place. Use lace as part of a gift to keep your love secure.

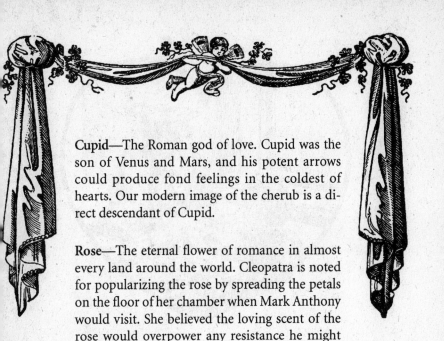

Cupid—The Roman god of love. Cupid was the son of Venus and Mars, and his potent arrows could produce fond feelings in the coldest of hearts. Our modern image of the cherub is a direct descendant of Cupid.

Rose—The eternal flower of romance in almost every land around the world. Cleopatra is noted for popularizing the rose by spreading the petals on the floor of her chamber when Mark Anthony would visit. She believed the loving scent of the rose would overpower any resistance he might have to her charms.

Birds—Old wives' tales tell us that birds choose their mates on Valentine's Day. Doves in particular are symbolic because they mate for life, and are considered a sign of fidelity.

Leaves—According to modern florists, leaves in an arrangement mean promises and hope from the giver.

Valentine's Day Divinations

By Patricia Telesco

A favorite pastime on Valentine's Day, even up to 100 years ago, was to attempt to predict whom one would marry. Here are some prophetic techniques to try:

Crack an egg into a bowl of water underneath the moon on Valentine's night. The shape of the white will indicate the occupation of your future love.

Spin a knife clockwise on the table before you. If it settles with blade toward you, your mate will be dark-haired; if away, he or she will be fair.

If you can catch a leaf (especially apple) before it hits the ground on Valentine's Day, the rest of the year will be happy for relationships.

English custom says if a bachelor places the whole plant "bachelor's button" in his pocket on Valentine's Day, and the plant continues to grow, he will be fortunate in matters of love.

To dream of your life partner, sprinkle two bay leaves with rose water and place them in a cross beneath your pillow. Alternatively, place one leaf on each of your bed posts and one on the center of the pillow.

Count buttons or beads on your shirt (daisy petals also work) to the old rhyme, "soldier, noble, sailor, lord, thief, tailor" to discover something unknown about the person of your heart's desire. This is also said to determine his or her trade.

If you place half of a four leaf clover in your shoe, the first person you meet thereafter is thought to bear the initials of the individual you will marry.

Look through the first keyhole you find on Valentine's Day. If you see a solitary object, the year will be spent without passionate companionship. More than one object, however, portends new friends and improved love prospects.

The Romantic Allure of Magical Scent

By Edain McCoy

Scent works on our most primal memory centers. Every odor which has wafted past our noses has been cataloged somewhere deep within our minds, and their return can prompt a rush of unexpected feelings and recollections. Likewise, provocative perfumes have been used throughout human history to tempt the opposite sex by arousing desire and sparking the embryonic flames of romance. The attempt was always to keep the fragrances unique so that when the chosen lover caught the scent for only a second, he or she would immediately be reminded of and long for their new-found mate.

Magical folk can make their own romance-attracting scents, which have the added boost of our personal magic working behind them. All it takes is some time, visualization, and the sincere desire to draw a new love into your life.

Blend all oil/perfume recipes in one-ounce eyedropper bottles of dark glass (ask for these at any pharmacy). This protects the integrity of the scent over the long-term, as well as allowing you to keep firm control of the amount used as you create them. Homemade perfumes are very potent!

Use 1/2 ounce of olive, almond, or saffron oil as the base. These are relatively scentless oils in which the essential oils you will be using will be able to disperse and "marry." Place all other oils (the essential oils) into the base, one careful drop at a time. Be sure to keep notes as you go along. You may wish to make changes in the formula later on, or you may accidentally create a blend you really love and, without the recipe, you will be unable to reproduce it. As you create your personal romance-inducing perfume, keep your visualization strong and your desire keen.

Perfume to Attract Men

1 drop rosemary oil
9 drops gardenia oil
3 drops rose oil
3 drops carnation oil
5 drops vanilla oil

Perfume to Attract Women

1 drop patchouly oil
9 drops orange oil
2 drops nutmeg oil
2 drops rosemary oil
2 drops clove oil

The Magic of Mardi Gras

By Edain McCoy

Mardi Gras, or "Fat Tuesday," is an ancient feast day celebrated on the day before the start of Lent (Ash Wednesday on the Christian calendar). Though the observance is native to early medieval France and Spain, it is now most deeply associated with New Orleans, a revelry-loving city which, for many years, was the primary French outpost in the New World. In the weeks before Fat Tuesday, the citizens of the city, and their visitors, host a never-ending orgy of drink, food, and masquerade in the city's quaint French Quarter.

Like most European festivals, Mardi Gras had its roots in the ancient Pagan world. In Rome, the pre-spring season was known as carnivale (the origin of our English word "carnival"), meaning "festival of meat." This was a magical time, not really winter and not yet spring, when the rules of society were turned upside down. Hiding behind masks, the low-born and high-born mingled and made merry without censor. In Germany, this period was known as Fasching, a word derived from an old German word meaning "flesh eating." Bizarre costumes were donned to frighten away any cold-loving evil spirits who might wish to prevent the coming of spring. The timing of these festivals during the most hungry time of the year, when the food stores of winter were running low, was no accident. The feast and frolic was an act of good faith in the deities who their followers were sure would provide them a bountiful hunt when the world thawed and game returned. Sometime around the twelfth century Mardi Gras entered the Christian calendar as the day just before Lent, a period of forty days when it is traditional to give up meat and other "extravagant" foods to commemorate the fast of Jesus just before his death.

Today, the carnival begins on Twelfth Night (January 6), known on the Christian calendar as the Epiphany (incidentally, Twelfth Night is a Norse Pagan observance) and continues until the stroke of midnight on Ash Wednesday.

The traditional colors of Mardi Gras are green, gold, and purple, symbolizing faith, power, and justice today as they did in Pagan Rome. The celebration is still characterized by prodigal consumption of food and drink, and lavish costume balls. During the carnival period, New Orleans is "ruled" by a collection of thinly disguised Pagan Kings and Lords of Misrule who distribute money charms intended to bring the recipients good fortune in the year to come.

Most of the native magic of New Orleans comes from the Carribean voodoo tradition, a blending of African deities and magic with Catholicism. These spells usually involve using the accoutrements of the dead.

A New Orleans Voodoo-Style Money Spell

Mix High John the Conqueror root with the dirt taken from an old graveyard after midnight. Before the light of day, tie up the mixture in a piece of cloth taken from the clothes of a corpse. Keep the charm, known in New Orleans as a gris-gris, in your left pocket. Money should soon come your way.

Traditional Mardi Gras Carnival Cake

On the first night of the festival, the ruler of the day is chosen when a traditional magical cake, known as King's Cake, is served. The cake, baked in the shape of a crown, is an old Pagan custom familiar to most Europeans. A single pecan is mixed into the batter, nuts being ancient and widespread symbols of abundance and fertility. The person finding the nut in his or her piece becomes the undisputed king or queen until sundown the following night. The next time you need to select a leader for a magickal gathering, try electing him or her through the magic of the King's Cake.

Recipe for Carnival King's Cake

1 egg, well-beaten with a tablespoon
   of rich milk
1/2 rounded cup granulated sugar
4 cups flour
1 teaspoon ground nutmeg
1/8 teaspoon allspice
2 tablespoons grated lemon
   or orange rinds
1/2 cup rich milk
5 egg yolks
1/4 cup butter (avoid margarine!)
1 teaspoon salt
1/2 cup warm water
1 package yeast
1 pecan or other nut

Pre-heat oven to 375°F and grease one regular-sized bundt pan. In a small bowl, mix the warm water, yeast, and a sprinkle of the sugar. Allow it to rest undisturbed for about fifteen minutes.

In a larger bowl, combine all other ingredients, adding the flour gradually one cup at a time to allow for easier mixing.

Add the yeast mixture and blend. Dough should be sticky, but not wet. You may add another 1/2 cup of flour if the dough seems too moist.

On a floured board, or in a buttered bowl, knead the dough until it becomes "shiny" and loses its tacky feeling. Place the dough in a deep bowl and cover it with a dish towel. Allow it to sit undisturbed in a warm place for one to two hours, or until nearly doubled in volume.

Knead again and place into bundt pan. With a pastry brush, brush a mixture of egg white, milk, and melted butter over the surface. Bake for 25 to 35 minutes, or until the surface is a golden brown.

Allow the cake to cool while the icing is being prepared. Traditionally, the icing is put on in alternating colors of green, gold, and purple. To make the icing, mix the appropriate commercial food colorings each with 1/8 cup granulated sugar, 1-1/2 cups confectioner's sugar, 1/8 scant teaspoon cinnamon or nutmeg, two tablespoons lemon or orange juice, and two tablespoons water.

March 15: The Festival of

Anna Perenna

By Edain McCoy

On the old Roman calendar, March was the first month of the year. On the Ides of March (now infamous as the date of the assassination of Julius Caesar), the Romans honored one of the world's oldest known deities—Anna Perenna, Goddess of new beginnings, vegetation, and fertility, whose Latin name means "returns yearly." Her day was characterized by joyous celebrations of the new spring, including communal games, feasting, and fertility rites. In return for their homage, Anna granted her followers an abundant harvest which would see them through to her next festival day.

Babe on a Broomstick: Aspecting Your Beauty Within

By Silver RavenWolf

All of us want to be beautiful, both inside and out. Being beautiful doesn't mean we have to look like the popular models of our times. It does mean taking care to satisfy our needs through grooming, personal health, and mental well-being. The first step is to learn to love ourselves in order to take care of these needs.

The following are magickal correspondences that will help you aspect the beauty within and without. Try using them to create ritual baths, sachets, dream pillows, or personal beauty rituals.

Planetary Vibrations

Sun: Health
Moon: Emotions and Dreams
Mars: Passion
Mercury: Wisdom and Healing
Venus: Romantic love, friendships, beauty

Days of the Week

Sunday: Health
Monday: Emotions, dreams
Tuesday: Passion
Wednesday: Wisdom, grace, and healing
Thursday: Business and money relationships
Friday: Love and friendships

Moons

Full: Romance and passion
New: Beginning beauty or fitness regimine
Waning: Removing bad habits
Moon in Leo: romance
Moon in Aries: Beginning new relationships
Moon in Libra: Beauty

Colors

Brown: Invoking friendship
Dark Purple: Calling ancient beauty
Dark Green: Invoking regeneration energies
Green: Invoking health
Lavender: Invoking outer beauty
Light Blue: Invoking inner beauty
Ruby Red: Invoking passion
Red: Romantic love
Silver: Invoking beauty of spirit

Planetary Hours

Hour of Venus: Love and natural beauty
Hour of the Sun: Self-healing
Hour of Mars: Passion
Hour of Mercury: Inner beauty and wisdom

Goddesses and Gods

Aphrodite: Cyprus, beauty and love
Isis: Egyptian, All-encompassing
Venus: Roman, Romantic love and beauty
Brighid: Celtic, Healing and the arts
Callisto: Greek, Beauty
Ashera: (Bride of Jehovah), Mother of Gods.

Aengus MacOg: Irish, young God of love
Apisiharts: Blackfoot Tribe, a Venus God
Apocatequil: Inca, God of regeneration
O-Kuni-Nushi: Japanese, God of medicine
Cernunnos: Celtic, sexual strength

Spell of Regeneration

From the void
I form myself
I spin the web
I weave the art
I bring joy and beauty to my heart.

Crystal Gazing and Scrying

By Patricia Telesco

It is another kind of perception, which is born in them and which is realized not by sight, but by the soul.

—Ibn Kaldoun 1332

Scrying as a means of divination is easily traceable to both Greek and Roman cultures, if not earlier. At these early junctures, scrying was done with water, polished metal, or other reflective surfaces. The use of crystal balls, however, emerged during the Middle Ages.

The Magi (priests of Zoroaster in Persia) were said to utilize golden spheres, etched with magical symbols and inlaid with a sapphire for a type of oracle. The orb was attached carefully to a piece of leather and twirled or spun while spells and incantations were recited. Beryl was the favorite stone to use for crystal gazing throughout this period, rather than the contemporary quartz stone. It was said that beryl could protect one from fascination or defeat by one's enemies.

There was tremendous divergence in opinion regarding the choice of a stone. John Dee preferred a deep red, while his contemporaries often suggested black.

Procedures to achieve visions were abundant. Sometimes a spell or invocation was spoken before the attempt. What is interesting is that several of these magical verses were very religious in nature, which reveals some tolerance of white magic by the Church. It seems, up until the 16th century, scrying abilities were regarded by some clergy as a special gift of God, given to those whose prayers and faith were ardent. Actually, it was often customary for a gentleman of means to have both a seer and a doctor in his employ.

Generally speaking, to try a crystal for gazing, it is suggested that one rinse it first in water to cleanse it from impurities, both physical and spiritual. If using beryl, working during the hour or moon sign of Libra is recommended, whereas quartz appears to function best with a waxing to full moon. Next, the crystal is placed on a cloth or stand, as your gaze is focused on one single point. Slowly you will notice your vision blurring and a slight haze will appear. It is from this foggy apparition that visions are said to come.

These images can be literal or symbolic. For instance, you might see an actual portrait of someone you're thinking about, or you could get a shape which is somehow emblematic of the answer to your question. Movement in the mists can also determine your answer. Left to right means negative, right to left positive, and circles mean no answer is readily available.

Discovering Dragons

By D.J. Conway

Have you ever worked magick in cooperation with a dragon? Do you want dragon friends and helpers? It's an exciting experience to know you have dragon-power backing your efforts, and it isn't that difficult to make their acquaintance. You just have to believe that dragons exist in the astral plane, and that they would like very much to become friends with you.

Dragons are the most fascinating of entities. They are powerful co-magicians, who have access to forgotten knowledge and untapped energies. Dragons must be dealt with honestly if the magician wishes to attract their help. Like many other beings, physical and non-physical, dragons will take advantage of anyone who vacillates in their commitment or is untruthful with them. Working with dragons is not a master-slave relationship, but one of partners.

I have never met an "evil" dragon, although I have encountered a few who distrust humans so much that one must take special care when working with them. Dragons become "evil" only where there is an imbalance of energies, a disruption of the powers flowing from the Earth and humans to dragons and back again. This imbalance came into existence when the Western world decided to believe that all dragons were evil and hateful. The Oriental world has always thought of their dragons as wise, powerful, perhaps a little tricky, but helpful.

Once maligned, Western dragons decided to live up to their reputation. Western magicians forgot how to work with dragons. Those who did contact their energies tried to order them about. This all backfired, and the dragons withdrew from most contact with the Western world and its inhabitants.

To coax back the dragons, Western magicians must reorganize their beliefs and thinking. We must be patient, willing to accept them as co-magicians, not slaves, and be ready to relearn much of the magick that history and religion buried long ago. Fortunately, this isn't too difficult. There are simple steps a magician can take to entice these great and powerful co-magicians back into her/his life.

It is possible to call dragons by singing musical notes or chanting the vowels in a musical tone. You don't have to have a trained voice or sing a specific sound. Dragons love music and singing. Through partnership with dragons the magician can learn to hear the music that emanates from all objects, animate and inanimate.

Dragons will be very understanding about your musical attempts. After all, some of their singing takes getting used to; it is very different from what we humans ordinarily hear. Each dragon has a very distinct, unique song or melody of its own, which it has developed as its identity-signature. They don't sing for just anyone, so recognize the honor you are being paid if your dragons share their songs with you.

Different species of dragons have different abilities and interests. Dragons connected with the element of fire, or those of fire and volcanoes, are most effective in tearing down impossible barriers and getting things moving. Creative and mental pursuits belong to the wind and air dragons. Earth dragons are interested in the

acquiring of material possessions and accomplishing goals. The dragons of water heal emotional pain, help to stabilize emotions, and will point you in the right direction to discover love and friendship.

All dragons will work together to improve spiritual enlightenment and growth. When the very foundation of magick and ritual is uncovered, the magician finds that all spell working is meant to be an eventual road to such growth and development. All realms of existence are connected through the spiritual plane. Everything in our physical plane must first be formed and imbued with life in the spiritual realm. Subconsciously, reaching for higher spiritual enlightenment is the goal of every true magician.

The first dragons you will probably attract are the little personal guardian dragons. They are less powerful than the huge dragons, and young and inexperienced in the art of magick. However, guardian dragons are more or less astral watch-dogs of both your property and your person, and they are great fun to have around. Usually they are quiet and invisible, at least to the senses of most people, but they can and do make disturbing noises and cause uncomfortable vibrations to those people they feel might cause their friends distress or harm. One of the easiest ways to communicate with these little entities is to invite them to join you in dancing.

Large dragons also love to dance. When they feel emotional about something, they move with the rhythms of the vibrations given off by that person or event.

Dragons can be found frolicking around young babies. They are expressing the joy of life, the vibrations of self-power and hope, the ecstasy of possibility. Their movements are totally uninhibited, expressive of every shade of their own emotions and those they feel emanating from the human.

A life-long dance with dragons is never boring. Dancing with dragons is a constant exploration of various types of energies and the uses to which they can be applied. Dragons will start you off in a kind of "kindergarten," where they will teach you how to manifest for physical needs. When they feel you are ready, they will teach you other forms of magick: healing, mental disciplines, emotional balance, and spiritual seeking. Just when you think you have learned everything about a subject, the dragons will surprise you with some hidden knowledge or a different method of magick.

Working with dragons can be a joyful experience, one eagerly sought and enjoyed by both the human and the dragons. The mutual sharing of energies and trust helps both species in their evolution. The more magicians who seek out the companionship of dragons, working with them and earning their trust, the more dragons will be encouraged to have a closer relationship with humans.

Open your heart, mind and soul to the possibilities of dragons and working with them. Dragons will crowd into your daily and ritual life, peering over your shoulder as you work. It is a wonderful experience.

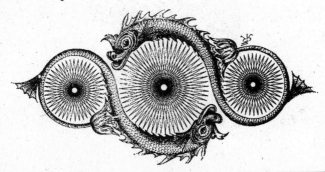

The Beginning

By Paul Harless

Shadows dance about me,
Prancing dancers
keeping beat
Withe the Exotic Steel drum,
that is   the rain.

Protecting and Purifying Potpourris
for Spring Cleaning

By Edain McCoy

There is more to having a clean house than just the physical absence of dust and debris. By using magical potpourris your house will not only be clean, but the vibrational field around it will be purified, and the area surrounding it well protected from both human and astral invaders.

Each potpourri you wish to make will require a small amount of dried or fresh herbs and/or flowers in pleasing combinations of scents; a small square of cotton or cheese-cloth fabric, cut in a circle about eight inches in diameter; and a few inches of colored ribbon with which to tie the bags shut. The color of the bag can be any which appeals to your inner senses. The ribbon tie can be of the same color, or of any other which catches your fancy.

The potpourris should be infused with your magical intent as you mix and make them. Mix all ingredients well, trying to "marry" the scent of the oils to the solid matter as much as possible. Continue visualizing as you stuff and tie the bags. They can then be hung above doors or windows, or placed discreetly in drawers around your house. Each time you catch their gentle scent, know that their magic is at work.

You can revive lost odor by adding a bit more oil, or by emptying the contents onto a cookie sheet and heating for a few minutes in a lukewarm oven.

Protection Potpourri #1

2 dozen cloves
3 drops cinnamon oil
3 bruised cinnamon sticks
4 sprigs fresh rosemary
small handful fresh pine needles

Protection Potpourri #2

3 dozen peppercorns
3 drops ginger oil
6 drops nutmeg oil
scant 1/4 cup dried orange peels
1 teaspoon dried rosemary

Purification Potpourri #1

1 tablespoon solid myrrh gum
1/4 cup dried sage
3 drops lemon oil
2 tablespoons fresh lavender
1 drop eucalyptus oil
1 drop frankincense oil

Purification Potpourri #2

3 drops ylang-ylang oil
6 bruised vanilla beans
1/4 cup dried or fresh rose petals
4 drops rose oil
6 drops vanilla extract

The Lore of 'Canis Familiaris'

By Edain McCoy

Today the dog is undisputably mankind's best friend, but in the not too distant past dogs were viewed with some suspicion. In Egypt, the jackal-headed God Anubis elevated canines to divine status. In Wales they were the ever-present companions of the death God Gwyn Ap Nuad, the hounds assisting him in his hunt for human souls. Several Irish heroes were named after dogs, including the famous warriors Curoi and Cuchulain.

A myriad of superstitions and folk beliefs are recorded about our "best friends." Some of these might seem silly to us. Others may affirm our deepest convictions that dogs are privy to information from worlds we normally cannot see. The following is a list of some of those beliefs:

- Scottish Highlanders believe that seeing Cu Sith, the black faery dog, run cross your path at night, foretells of your death within a fortnight.

- In western Europe, white dogs are believed to be the familiars of faery folk.

- If a faery dog barks within human hearing it is a sign of coming death.

- In Cornwall, the hounds of the Horned God, Herne, are called "Wishing Hounds." When they are heard galloping over Dartmoor Heath, the local children close their eyes and make wishes.

- To the Native Americans, dogs were seen as feral creatures. The coyote was the elemental embodiment of the unexpected, earning the nickname "Trickster."

- In ancient Israel, dogs were symbols of fidelity and protection. They were painted on marriage contracts and carved into city gateposts.

- If a dog growls at an empty space it means that a ghost treads there.

- Catching a dog's tail in the door when it is exiting your home is an ill omen, and a sign that you should remain home until the next daybreak.

- In Persia, the dog was considered to be a bringer of illness. They were also associated with "black magic." Anyone owning a dog could be charged with the "crime" of Witchcraft.

Handling the Magickal Emergency

By Silver RavenWolf and MaraKay Rogers

Instant magickal remedies won't help you if you have not put in the practice required. That means for them to work properly, you need experience. Experience does not mean length of service in the Craft, the degree you hold, or even the amount of time you've spent with your nose in grimoires. It depends upon the amount of hands-on magick you have done with success, the number of rituals you have performed accurately, and your confidence in your everyday performance.

Intent is the key factor. Have your intent firmly in your mind before you start. You also must be able to hold on to it for a period of time. This is what all your practice in meditation and visualization was for in the beginning of your studies. Here is where your hard work pays off.

Do not limit yourself needlessly. This means leave the solutions open-ended and concentrate on the final goal.

Keep talking, as long as you have some idea of what you are saying. Hopefully, you have memorized a few all-purpose spells, rhymes, or chants. This will help to trigger the specifics of the matter. The specifics don't have to be beautiful, or memorized in advance, they don't need to rhyme, in fact they may have no tonal beat at all. That's acceptable, as long as you keep focused.

Yes, you can cast a circle in your head, just be sure that you do cast it and visualize its presence. At this stage, you should be able to picture yourself walking about and casting it, hearing yourself saying the words. If you need cue cards, forget it.

Use the poem entitled The Witches' Rune by Doreen Valiente, and learn it by heart. There is no excuse not to memorize it. It should not go out of your head in a crisis, but rather, it should be ready for instant recall.

If you can visualize a circle, you can also draw down by fixing the intent firmly and seeing the process while taking a few deep breaths. The same with aspecting. Remember a ritual where you did both or one of these things. How did it feel? What sensations did you have at that time? This is the feeling/sensation you are going for now, without the props.

You don't have tools? Have you got at least one hand? Hands point as well as fingers and knives; they hold water, like a chalice or cauldron; they are solid matter, like the earth; they are consecrated by being part of your own body.

Above all: Don't Panic. There is no magickal problem that you can't fix somehow as long as you can think straight. This is not as easy as you first would think. Take time now to recall instances when you panicked and when you didn't. Practice now the act of going into alpha when panic is headed your way. You won't regret it.

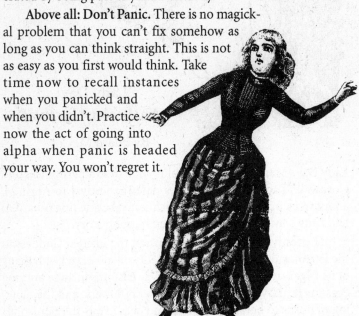

Lady Day:
An Ancient Festival

By Edain McCoy

Lady Day (March 25) is a festival unique to southern Wales and Cornwall. Though some sources date the festival to April 24, about week prior to Beltaine, which festival came first is hard to tell. Lady Day's origins are lost deep in pre-history.

The festival celebrates the return of the maiden Goddess to the Earth, and in modern Cornwall it is still observed with many of its Pagan attributes intact. Lady Day customs include burying eggs for fertility, decorating homes with flowers, and the blowing of horns to herald the spring and chase away the elementals of winter.

Mothers who give birth on Lady Day are thought to be especially blessed. In the not too distant past the afterbirth was taken by the mother to one of the ancient standing stone formations and laid at the base as an offering to the Goddess. Though this custom has died out, the day is still considered an auspicious one on which to be born.

Pagan Lady Day rituals emphasize the maiden aspect of the Goddess as she searches for her Lord Consort. Because of this eternal quest for love, it is not surprising that romantic divinations became part of the holiday. Young women particularly like to scry into pools of water while drinking milk, or plucking the blossoms off flowering primrose in hopes of catching a glimpse of their unknown true loves.

A Cornish circle dance popular on Lady Day further ties in with the theme of discovering the unknown lover by having all the unmarried women form one circle, and the unmarried men form another one inside the women's. Music is played as the two formations skip in opposite directions: the women counterclockwise, and the men clockwise. When the music stops, the person standing opposite is the designated partner for the next dance set, and sometimes for the feasting also.

Vestiges of Lady Day fertility rites can also be seen in modern Cornwall as those who wish to conceive in the year ahead go, as did their ancestors, to the stone formation known as Men-an-Tol. This is a large upright holey stone, representative of the birth canal, which sits next to a tall projective standing stone, which functions as a phallic symbol. The women pass themselves nine times sunwise through the holey stone while chanting charms to enhance their personal fertility.

As a joyous spring festival, Lady Day has changed little over the past thousand years, proving that once people have found a good thing, they are loathe to part with it. May the Lady be reunited with her beloved Lord for many, many more Lady Days to come!

The Pagan Past of Ireland's Oldest Symbol

By Edain McCoy

The wee little shamrock, the tiny trefoil clover of vivid green which grows in abundance on the Emerald Isle, has a long and cherished Pagan history, as well as a legacy of magical uses.

Modern Irish lore tells us it was St. Patrick who bought the shamrock to notice by likening it to the Holy Christian Trinity of Father, Son, and Holy Ghost. Long before he catapulted the shamrock into prominence as Ireland's principal emblem, it was honored as the symbol of the powerful Triple Goddess: the Maiden, Mother, and Crone—three separate deities, yet one. In Irish mythology, the shamrock is linked to three important Goddesses: Airmid, a Goddess of herbal healing; Eire, the Goddess for whom Ireland is named; and Dechtere, who alternately takes on the images of Maiden, Mother, and Crone throughout her myths.

As a magical herb, the shamrock (*seamrog* in Irish) has been used for a host of beneficial purposes. To add a touch of Irish luck to your magic, try any of these ideas:

♣ Use the little trefoil as a focus to help you align with or invoke the Triple Goddess.

♣ The shamrock can be used as a catalyst for magical healing by helping you draw on the powers of the Goddess of medicine, Airmid.

♣ Fresh shamrocks are irresistible to friendly faeries. Irish lore tells us they also make great bait for capturing Leprechauns.

♣ The white variety of shamrock makes a superb protective talisman when carried or sewn up into protective charms.

♣ Shamrocks can be set in windows to psychically purify the room and protect the window.

♣ The verdant green of shamrocks makes them a natural in money/prosperity or fertility spells. You can efficaciously replace any other herbs in these spells with shamrocks.

♣ Carry shamrocks in your pocket when going on a job interview to give you a leg up in the job hunting process. (But beware! They may also bestow upon you the gift of Blarney.)

♣ The shamrock is the origin of the belief about four-leaved clovers being lucky. If you find a four leaved shamrock—a rare mutation—you should make a wish. Then bury the sprig, sealing the spell in the earth by making three clockwise circles above it.

♣ Most of all, shamrocks are very, very lucky...ever heard of the "Luck o' the Irish?"

How the Gods Stole Back the Spring
An Anglo-Saxon Myth

Retold by Edain McCoy

Once upon a time, when the world and all its Gods were young, there lived a giant named Wandil who loved winter. He cared not for the human suffering and deprivation caused by the harsh cold, and he laughed at their prayerful pleas for their Spring Goddess's return.

One winter, Wandil decided to steal the spring so that the world would be forced to remain in winter forever. Unknown to the other deities, he stole the Spring Goddess and buried her.

The seasons passed, and soon it was again time for spring. The people gathered in the snow for their ritual welcoming the Goddess of Spring back to the Earth. They waited and waited, but she never came. The Earth remained frozen, and only the other Gods and Goddesses knew that the Goddess of Spring was imprisoned in the Underworld by Wandil, where her people's cries could not reach her.

The Sun God tried timidly to make his return to the earth, to sneak in when Wandil was not looking, hoping he could get close enough to melt the ice which sealed his beloved spring bride in her Underworld prison. But Wandil was a cautious old beast, and whenever he felt the telltale warmth of the Sun God's approach, he would huff and puff and blast the Sun with his chilling breath, sending him scurrying away again.

The other deities were growing worried. Their people were starving. Without the new vegetation and the return of the herds, they would soon perish. Finally they knew they had to take action, and they conspired to attack Wandil as one, sure that their combined strength could rid the Earth of the cold giant forever.

One cold winter's night, when Wandil was enjoying a stroll in the frigid night air, the deities mounted their attack and, together, landed him a blow which was so powerful that it knocked Wandil right off the Earth and far out into the dark heavens.

The deities, surprised at the force of their combined strength, watched in wonder as two twin stars appeared high in the heavens. There they blinked, as if startled, and then they came to rest. With the giant gone, the Sun God returned to the Earth and released his bride from her long burial, and all the people and the deities rejoiced.

But Wandil watches and waits for the time he can return to steal away spring once more. Look up on any clear winter's night and you will see him. The twin stars we know today as Castor and Pollux will be shining down on you. You can rest assured that it will be a frosty night when the earth lies under Wandil's unobstructed glare.

April Fool's Day: The Lord of Misrule Rides Again

By Edain McCoy

In the Middle Ages, when New Year's Day was moved from March to January 1, there was considerable confusion among people over just when the new year began. Those who clung to the old time reckoning, or who just plain forgot or refused to switch, were called "April's Fools." Throughout western Europe a custom developed of playing tricks and practical jokes on unsuspecting friends and family on this day, which is still in force today. In modern America, Wiccans have adopted this day as their own, allowing the Lord of Misrule to reign supreme for a second day in the year.

Calling In Minerva: Three Witches
Experience Aspecting

By Silver RavenWolf

The last of the ladies gave their good-byes. A cold blast of wind tore through the room as the door banged shut. I leaned back on my chair, tipping it slightly to allow myself a good stretch. The candles in the middle of the dining room table guttered in protest, their night of magick nearly spent. The three of us gazed at each other through bleary eyes.

I flicked an errant potato chip crumb across the table cloth. The effort of lifting my fingernail to do the deed was more than I'd anticipated. "These evenings keep getting longer and longer," I muttered.

"We had quite a crew tonight," said MaraKay. "I think there were over eighteen people here."

"I have so much to do next week. I don't know where I'm going to find the time," moaned Diane.

Monsters unbidden, like deadlines, correspondence, errands,

and appointments rose from our collective unconscious, swirling above our heads. Their spectral hideousness got caught in the cobwebs of my dining room. Better add housecleaning to that list.

"I don't know where to begin," I said sourly.

"I say we do some aspecting!" MaraKay announced.

I looked about the room, taking in the kitchen with pained eyes. An hour's worth of clean-up, my mind giggled hysterically — let alone the cottony mounds of cobwebs reproducing themselves in every corner of my house. "So, whom do we aspect? It better be good," I said.

"Ah, I know the one!" announced MaraKay, "Minerva!"

"Who's Minerva?" I asked.

"Wasn't she a Roman goddess?" asked Diane.

"Precisely," said MaraKay, "and I think she is our ticket."

"Tell me more about Minerva," I prodded.

MaraKay smiled magnanimously. "She is indeed a Roman Goddess. Her persona merged with the Greek goddess Athene early in her career. Minerva was a protectress of commerce, education, and enterprise. She's a mover and a shaker, helping you get your motor running. She pulls in creativity and cuts short the habit of procrastination."

"Sounds good to me," said Diane. "I need something to get me moving, particularly at the moment."

Like all deities, Minerva has correspondences and associations that are particular to Her — items like dragonsblood, horns, magickal weapons and tiger lilies. I had three of the four, not bad for spur-of-the moment work. With the cauldron in the middle of the table, flanked by stag horns and our athames, we were nearly ready. The candle flame in the center of the cauldron flickered rapidly as I poured a small circle of dragonsblood around its base. It reminded me of a heartbeat infused with adrenalin.

"Let's stand and hold hands," said MaraKay quietly.

Breathing deeply, we shut our eyes and listened to MaraKay's sing-song voice. Each of us imagined the Goddess Minerva descending upon the room, moving into our circle, and through our bodies. Each of us asked Her to instill us with the energies needed to deal with the forthcoming week. My most prominent memory of the experience was of the color gold, much like a flashing, tempered shield.

The following week brought about accomplishments and opportunities — some I had not anticipated, others concluded right on schedule. In all honesty, I finished several main projects long before their deadlines. It had been a good week. In the rush, I forgot about our aspecting session.

Our meeting night rolled around. Amidst the laughter and chatter that accompanies everyone when they arrive, Diane sought me out, dragging me to the kitchen. "I don't know about you," she said, "but that aspecting thing we did really worked for me! I got more done in one week than I have accomplished in the last month! That was great!"

We waited for MaraKay to arrive. She, too, related experiences much like ours. Among the three of us we had accomplished more than ten people. I only forgot one small task — the cobwebs.

Strange Animal Superstitions

By D. J. Conway

- Wrap a spider in a raisin and swallow it. This was an old remedy for chills and fever.

- Carrying a badger's tooth in your pocket will bring you good luck at cards and gambling.

- Anoint the bald spots on your head with goose dung, and hair will grow again.

- If you kill a wren, you will soon break a bone.

- Blue jays spend every Friday with the devil, reporting sins.

- In Britain, they say that a pillow made of pigeon feathers will prolong the life of a dying person.

- Turn the money over in your pocket when you hear a cuckoo call for the first time in the year. Then you will have more than enough money.

- To kill a beetle is to court bad luck.

- To kill a cricket is unlucky. One in the house brings good luck. Yorkshire.

- Hares change their sex yearly.

- Butterflies are the souls of the dead waiting to pass through Purgatory. Ireland.

- At birth, brush an infant with a rabbit's foot to avert all accidents.

- Hares found in the fields among cattle on May Day are witches stealing the milk. Ireland.

- In England to see a black cat cross the road is lucky.

- In parts of Yorkshire, England, the wives of fishermen keep black cats at home to ensure their husbands' safety at sea.

- A black lamb brings luck to the flock. England.

- To cure a man of drunkenness, put a live eel in his drink.

- In both Scotland and England it was said that goats are never seen for 24 hours straight because they visit to the Devil to have their beards combed.

- The ghosts of dogs walk around on St. John's Eve, but are seen only by other dogs.

- In the Highlands of Scotland, some people wear the teeth of mice as good luck charms.

- Hair taken from a specific area on the rump of a live wolf is said to be an aphrodisiac.

- The tails of horses were originally plaited with ribbons to keep the horse safe from witches.

- Many cultures believed that spirits of the dead took the form of bats. Therefore, a house with bats in it was haunted.

- A bat hitting a building is a sure sign of rain. It's certainly a sure sign of headache for the bat.

The Minor Magicks

By Silver RavenWolf

All the minor magicks require that you:

- ✪ Determine the moon phase and aspect that best suits the operation.

- ✪ Determine the day of the week that best suits the operation.

- ✪ Determine the hour of the day that best suits the operation.

- ✪ Know the deity associated with your choices and need and invoke or aspect that energy.

- ✪ Cleanse, consecrate, and empower all supplies and tools.

- ✪ Be proficient in raising and focusing energy.

⭐ **Petition Magick** is the easiest form of magick. It requires a piece of paper, a sacred space and the dolmen (altar). Petition magick is used for both minor and major problems, and can be used with other magickal applications without interference, as long as your focus and deity system remain the same. Petition magick is a very simple operation. Go to your altar, write down the situation, burn some incense, ask for guidance, and put the paper in the middle of the altar. You will get an answer.

Petition magick is good for problems in which you choose not to use any other type of magickal application. Perhaps you feel that throwing magick at a problem will not solve it and seek the correct direction in which to move. The petition should be burned after the answer is received and thanks given to the deity.

⭐ **Simple Mind Programming** is one of the easiest operations to do, but it is a lot of work on your part. Rather than raising energy and casting things off to the unknown, your objective is carefully planned and worked on during your daily meditation. The better you get at simple mind programming, the greater rate of success you will have at more difficult magickal applications.

Simple mind programming can be used in tandem with more difficult magickal operations. Meditation programming is very simple. Go into alpha and picture the situation as it now stands. Move the picture to the left and change it to the desired outcome. If you like, add a picture in the middle of the mundane things you know you can do to bring the desired outcome. During the next meditation procedure, do not again outline the problem or situation. Instead concentrate on either the outcome or the mundane actions and the outcome. Change the mundane applications as the desired result grows closer.

✭ **Candle Magick** works on three principles: The color of the candle; the type of oil used to dress it; and the sigils carved on it (or the paper put underneath it). To determine what color you should use, see the table that has been provided in this lesson. To determine what oil you should use, start with an inexpensive set of three (clove, cinnamon, and sandalwood)to make it easier. If you feel you need to use sigils, either check in your BOS or make one up. Sigils are easily melted into the candle with a hot needle, seam ripper, or nail.

Candle magick is very versatile and will often be used by adepts simply to center and focus. Most often used in candle magick are black candles to ward off negativity, and the fire candles in Pow-Wow applications. Remember that a white candle is considered all-purpose.

✭ **Cord Magick** is another simple magickal operation that can be used together with mind programming, candle magick, and petitioning. Cord magick entails the following: choice of cord color; charm or chant. The cord must be thirteen inches long and the order of knots is as follows: 1, 6, 4, 7, 3, 8, 5, 9, 2.

Cord magick requires the magickal operation of charging. Each knot is charged as the charm or chant is recited. Disposal of the cord depends upon the spell. If it is to banish negativity, you would bury the cord immediately. If it is for a healing or drawing something toward you, keep the cord until the job is done, then release the magick and burn the cord.

There are two types of cord and knot magick. The first is listed above; the second deals with Traditional Witches and accessing the group mind. Traditional witches can link their initiation cords together in a ritual setting to manifest a desired end. When the result has been achieved, the cords are taken apart and returned to their respective owners.

★Gem Magick includes work with crystals, gems, and precious stones. It can be used in conjunction with any of the aforementioned magickal operations. Gem magick entails the following: choice of gem and programming of the stone. This is the first magickal operation where a bit of study and experimentation before you begin any serious working should be contemplated.

Magickal applications are light for this operation, such as creating a good environment (rose quartz); getting rid of negativity (amethyst); protection (smokey quartz); etc. Certain gems can be mixed together to make a tuned operation. For example you could carry rose quartz and amethyst together. Be careful which stones you mix and match. They are like people and some of them refuse to work together.

Every Witch should carry two lode stones: One to draw things toward you and one to dispel psychic attacks, break negative shields, and ward off negativity.

★Elemental Magick employs the elements, including the sylphys, gnomes, undines, and salamanders, which equate to earth, air, water, and fire. The fifth element is spirit. Elemental magicks can range from simple (burning a piece of paper and tossing it in the wind, using earth-paper, air-wind, and of course, the fire) to a more complicated ritual. Elemental is often called "practical magick" because it uses things most common to your environment.

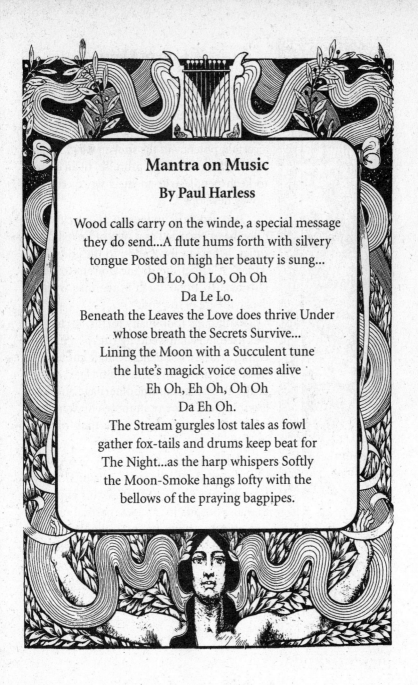

Mantra on Music

By Paul Harless

Wood calls carry on the winde, a special message
they do send...A flute hums forth with silvery
tongue Posted on high her beauty is sung...
Oh Lo, Oh Lo, Oh Oh
Da Le Lo.
Beneath the Leaves the Love does thrive Under
whose breath the Secrets Survive...
Lining the Moon with a Succulent tune
the lute's magick voice comes alive
Eh Oh, Eh Oh, Oh Oh
Da Eh Oh.
The Stream gurgles lost tales as fowl
gather fox-tails and drums keep beat for
The Night...as the harp whispers Softly
the Moon-Smoke hangs lofty with the
bellows of the praying bagpipes.

A Cup of Unity

By Patricia Telesco

Our ancestors knew that people are not always honest. They also knew that there was a certain potency in the spoken word, especially when declaring a promise. In an effort to keep people true to their word, rituals slowly developed.

Two people drinking out of one cup has often been regarded as a sign of linked destinies. When an invocation to the gods was added, it called the divine powers to bear witness. To break such a promise would evoke the ire of the gods!

Oath cups took many forms. A chalice was used in Pagan wedding rites as a public demonstration of oneness. Single cups were passed clockwise in many Celtic feast gatherings to display common heritage and fellowship. In Germany a minne cup was given to a young couple to mark their pledge of love.

In Norse mead halls a horn or cup was often passed to guests as sign of fidelity from host to visitor. To refuse this cup was to refuse hospitality, and was basically an insult akin to saying the householder could not insure the guests' safety. Conversely, to accept the beverage was a way of saying that the guests would extend the same courtesies to their host.

A Lusty Brew for Beltaine

By Edain McCoy

Most Pagans are familiar with meade, the rich honey ale long linked to ancient spring fertility rites. Yet beyond the European world is an entire planet full of magical heritages that also have their special brews sacred to those randy times of the year. From a Polynesian tradition comes this lusty tropical beverage; a delicious blend of old ways and new.

 1 liter ginger ale
 1 pound honey
 1 cup orange juice
 2 cups pineapple juice
 1 cup passion fruit juice
 1/2 cup lime juice
 1/2 cup papaya juice
 1 cup alcohol of choice for
  "spiking" (optional)
 1 spacious punch bowl

In a medium-sized sauce pan, blend the honey and the orange juice over medium heat. Keep stirring until the honey is completely blended into the liquid. If you can still feel "heaviness" in the bottom of the pan, keep stirring. Remove from heat and allow to cool completely. In another bowl, combine remaining ingredients. Pour honey mixture into the punch bowl over crushed ice or ice cubes. Add the rest of the ingredients and mix well.

May 9, 11, and 13: The Ancient Festival of Lumeria

By Edain McCoy

Do you enjoy feeling the closeness of the spirit world? Are the feasts of the dead in October and November something you look forward to all year? Then include the Roman festival of Lumeria on your ritual calendar. Lumeria honors the lemures, the earth-wandering spirits of passed-over family members who return to the earth on these three spring nights. Be sure to prepare a meal in their honor if you wish to engender their continued good will.

Faery Sweet Breads

By Patricia Telesco

On April 30th, people baked sweet breads and left them outdoors to welcome the Wee Folk. If the breads were eaten, it was regarded as good fortune for the family, because their token to the fairies was accepted.

2 cups sifted flour
1 cup candied fruits
1 egg
1/2 teaspoon baking powder
1 cup buttermilk
1/2 cup honey
1 tablespoon rose water

Combine the flour, egg, baking powder, rose water, and buttermilk in a good-sized bowl, stirring until they are well blended. Next, fold in the candied fruits so they are distributed evenly in the dough. If the dough seems sticky, add more flour until you can work it easily with your fingers.

Shape heaping tablespoonfuls of the dough into four leaf clovers. Place on a greased cookie sheet at 350°F for about 10 minutes, until fully raised and slightly browned. Drizzle a little honey on top while cooling.

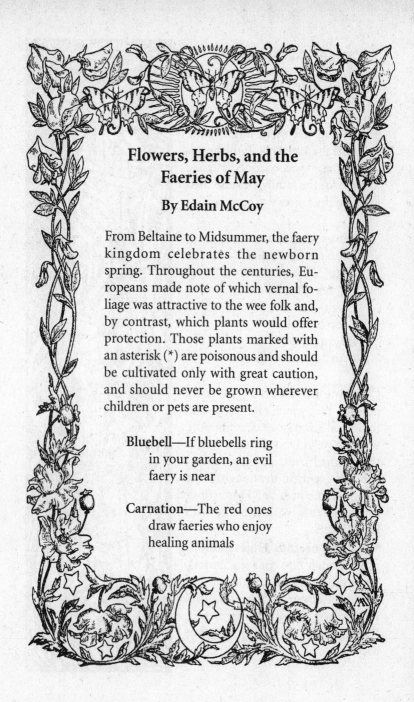

Flowers, Herbs, and the Faeries of May

By Edain McCoy

From Beltaine to Midsummer, the faery kingdom celebrates the newborn spring. Throughout the centuries, Europeans made note of which vernal foliage was attractive to the wee folk and, by contrast, which plants would offer protection. Those plants marked with an asterisk (*) are poisonous and should be cultivated only with great caution, and should never be grown wherever children or pets are present.

Bluebell—If bluebells ring in your garden, an evil faery is near

Carnation—The red ones draw faeries who enjoy healing animals

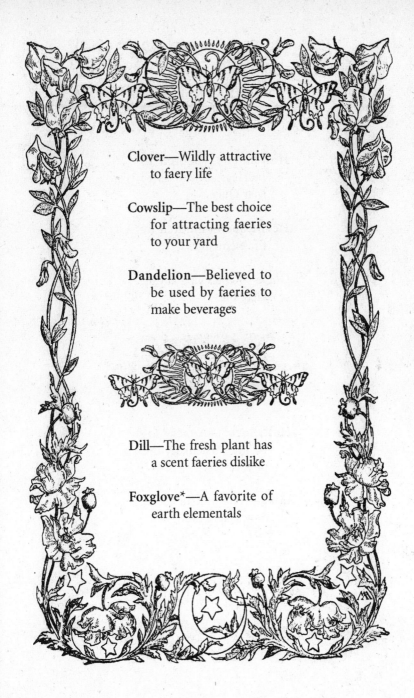

Clover—Wildly attractive to faery life

Cowslip—The best choice for attracting faeries to your yard

Dandelion—Believed to be used by faeries to make beverages

Dill—The fresh plant has a scent faeries dislike

Foxglove*—A favorite of earth elementals

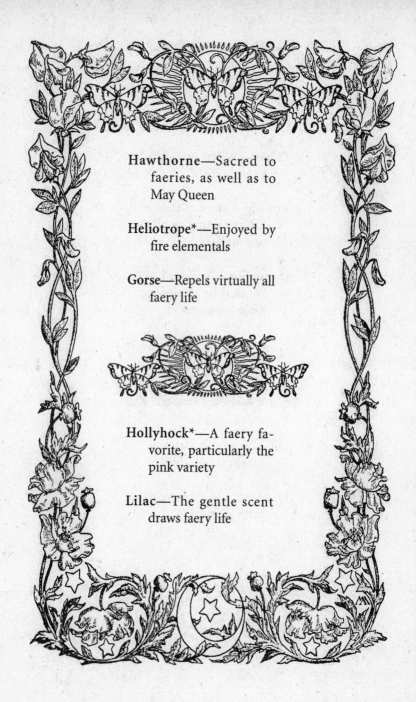

Hawthorne—Sacred to faeries, as well as to May Queen

Heliotrope* —Enjoyed by fire elementals

Gorse—Repels virtually all faery life

Hollyhock* —A faery favorite, particularly the pink variety

Lilac—The gentle scent draws faery life

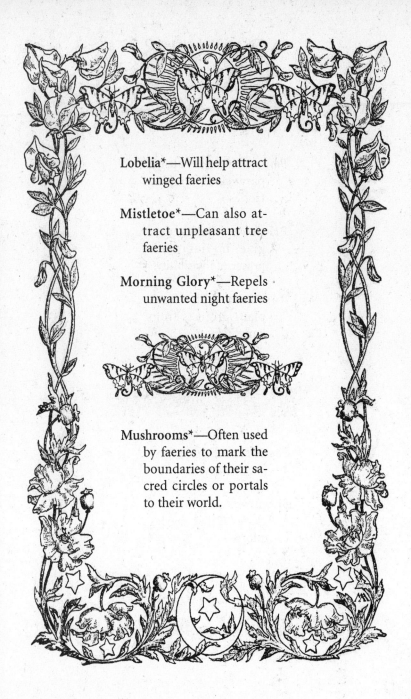

Lobelia*—Will help attract winged faeries

Mistletoe*—Can also attract unpleasant tree faeries

Morning Glory*—Repels unwanted night faeries

Mushrooms*—Often used by faeries to mark the boundaries of their sacred circles or portals to their world.

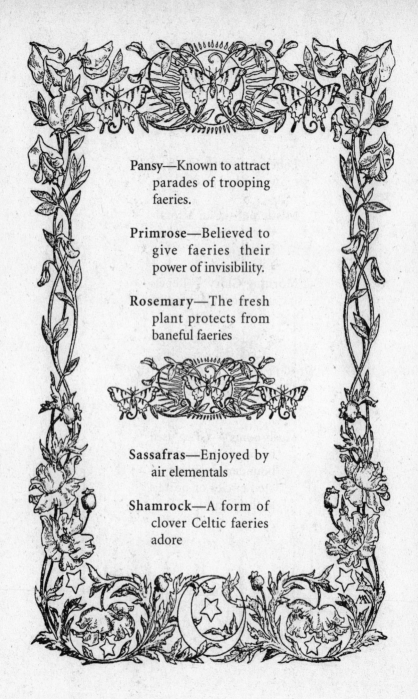

Pansy—Known to attract parades of trooping faeries.

Primrose—Believed to give faeries their power of invisibility.

Rosemary—The fresh plant protects from baneful faeries

Sassafras—Enjoyed by air elementals

Shamrock—A form of clover Celtic faeries adore

Almanac 2

Oils for Attuning
with the Elements

By Edain McCoy

As most magical folk are well aware, each of the four alchemical elements has its own sphere of influence. Ritual oils, each constructed with a single element in mind, can be worn, rubbed onto candles, burned as an incense, or used to anoint other magical catalysts in order to help us achieve our spiritual and magical goals.

All oil recipes should be mixed into a base of 1/2 ounce olive or saffron oil. Blend the scents by turning the bottle gently rather than

using a stirring tool. This avoids contamination of the compound from both physical and psychic impurities. Essential oils can be purchased through catalogs and at some health food stores.

Elemental Water Oil

Water is the realm of hidden mysteries, psychic senses, and peace.

12 drops sweet pea
4 drops jasmine
7 drops camellia
4 drops lotus

Elemental Earth Oil

Earth is the realm of of fertility, wealth, abundance, and stability.

1 drop patchouly
2 drops pine
13 drops magnolia
10 drops honeysuckle

Elemental Air Oil

Air is the sphere of the intellect, reason, new beginning, and change.

3 drops benzoin
12 drops lavender
9 drops lily of the valley

Elemental Fire Oil

Fire is associated with transformation, passion, leadership, and personal success.

    3 drops cinnamon
    12 drops orange
    2 drops clove
    7 drops nutmeg

Elemental Spirit Oil

The fifth element is spirit. It unifies all the other elements and is part of each of them. It is the realm of the divine, of spirituality, and of all the unseen worlds and their many inhabitants.

    8 drops sandalwood
    8 drops violet
    5 drops crocus
    5 drops gardenia

From The Scent Shop

By Patricia Telesco

Herbalism is one of the wonderful crafts re-emerging in our society. From simmering potpourri and aromatic baths to skin cream and herbal tea, the spices in our pantry racks are quickly adapting themselves for hundreds of practical or magical applications.

Herbal products are natural, are not harmful to the environment, and commonly cost far less to make than commercially purchased merchandise. The additional benefit is the ability to choose your ingredients according to their magical symbolism. Here are two examples for you to try:

Powder of Romance

I cup corn starch
3 tablespoons powdered rose petals
1 teaspoon powdered lemon rind
1 teaspoon powdered orange rind
2 teaspoons vanilla extract

Sift the cornstarch before scenting it. Add powdered rose petals. A good alternative to dried petals is two teaspoons of rose water. Add the lemon and orange powder (which can also be made in a good food grinder) along with the vanilla and stir well. Resift the entire mixture, then allow it to dry in open air. Store in an airtight container, applying as desired to bring love into your life.

Timing: Work during the Full Moon to help romantic feelings grow.

Other aromatics for love: cinnamon, clove, apple, basil, gardenia, geranium, ginger, jasmine, lavender, lotus, marjoram, peppermint, rosemary, thyme. Any of these can be added or substituted in your recipe. Be certain they are in powdered form so they are pleasant when applied to the skin.

Hint: If you have them, use drops of aromatic oil instead of powdered herbs. This makes a much softer powder.

Alternatives: Baking soda can be added to this recipe to help alleviate unseemly odors. Also, ground soapstone, when prepared with a rasp, sifted, and scented is a non-carcinogenic version of talc, and much silkier.

Bug Bane (for outdoor fires)

    1 cup dried mint leaf, preferably pennyroyal
    1 cup dried pine needles
    1 cup dried sage
    1 cup shaved cedar
    I cup dried marigold petals
    1 cup dried tomato leaves

Mix ingredients together and keep in an air-tight container. Sprinkle on your outdoor fires in 1/4 cup increments as needed to keep bugs away.

Timing: Prepare during a waning to New Moon to help turn insects away.

The Birthday Rattle

By Silver RavenWolf

Collect several gourds ranging in size. Allow them to dry thoroughly. Choose one that will become your birthday rattle. It should have a good strong rattle and aesthetically delight you. Paint the rattle a dark color. With a lighter color (silver, gold, white) paint tiny stars or moons to represent each year of your life. If you like, you can add feathers, beads, or ribbons to your creation.

On your birthday, make a wish and shake the rattle first thing in the morning. Throughout the day, shake the rattle as many times as you want, envisioning your wish. Before you go to bed, paint on another star or moon and shake the rattle again. Ask the energy of the universe to grant your wish.

Give birthday rattles as unique gifts to anyone. Design a card with instructions on using the magickal rattle. These rattles can also serve as Wiccaning gifts.

June 15: A Feast of Vestalia

By Edain McCoy

On this date in old Rome, the great temple of Vesta was closed, and the Goddess's handmaidens freed from their sacred duties so that community could come together to celebrate the first fruits of the harvest season. Vesta was a goddess of fire, the home, and cooking. She was also the patron goddess of women, and at her temple her sacred fires were tended by the six selected Vestal Virgins. These women were granted an independence and status rarely granted to other females under the Roman Empire.

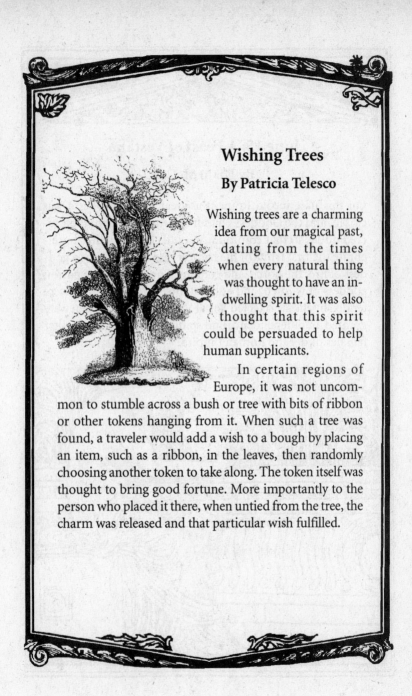

Wishing Trees

By Patricia Telesco

Wishing trees are a charming idea from our magical past, dating from the times when every natural thing was thought to have an indwelling spirit. It was also thought that this spirit could be persuaded to help human supplicants.

In certain regions of Europe, it was not uncommon to stumble across a bush or tree with bits of ribbon or other tokens hanging from it. When such a tree was found, a traveler would add a wish to a bough by placing an item, such as a ribbon, in the leaves, then randomly choosing another token to take along. The token itself was thought to bring good fortune. More importantly to the person who placed it there, when untied from the tree, the charm was released and that particular wish fulfilled.

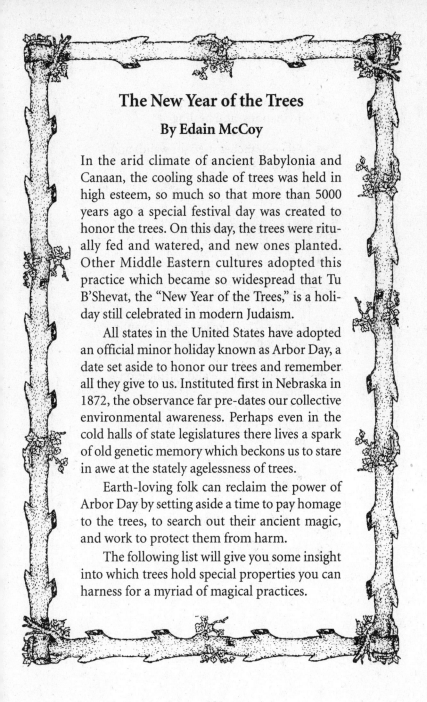

The New Year of the Trees

By Edain McCoy

In the arid climate of ancient Babylonia and Canaan, the cooling shade of trees was held in high esteem, so much so that more than 5000 years ago a special festival day was created to honor the trees. On this day, the trees were ritually fed and watered, and new ones planted. Other Middle Eastern cultures adopted this practice which became so widespread that Tu B'Shevat, the "New Year of the Trees," is a holiday still celebrated in modern Judaism.

All states in the United States have adopted an official minor holiday known as Arbor Day, a date set aside to honor our trees and remember all they give to us. Instituted first in Nebraska in 1872, the observance far pre-dates our collective environmental awareness. Perhaps even in the cold halls of state legislatures there lives a spark of old genetic memory which beckons us to stare in awe at the stately agelessness of trees.

Earth-loving folk can reclaim the power of Arbor Day by setting aside a time to pay homage to the trees, to search out their ancient magic, and work to protect them from harm.

The following list will give you some insight into which trees hold special properties you can harness for a myriad of magical practices.

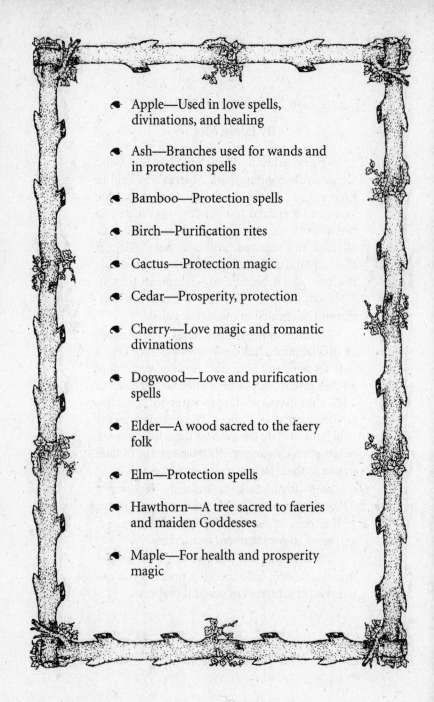

- Apple—Used in love spells, divinations, and healing

- Ash—Branches used for wands and in protection spells

- Bamboo—Protection spells

- Birch—Purification rites

- Cactus—Protection magic

- Cedar—Prosperity, protection

- Cherry—Love magic and romantic divinations

- Dogwood—Love and purification spells

- Elder—A wood sacred to the faery folk

- Elm—Protection spells

- Hawthorn—A tree sacred to faeries and maiden Goddesses

- Maple—For health and prosperity magic

- Mesquite—For healing magic

- Oak—Used in spells for stamina, lust, and fertility

- Orange—For gaining wisdom and employment

- Peach—Love magic

- Poplar—As an aid in astral projection

- Rowan—Used as a psychic enhancer and for healing magic

- Willow—Used in love, healing, and fertility

Tree Folklore

By Mary Brown

When we "touch wood," we may not realise it, but we are using the last remnant of ancient belief in the power of the Tree Gods. Every ancient culture had its gods who lived in sacred groves, and who had to be placated before the trees could be used for fuel, building, or tools. It is said that at one time a squirrel could travel the length of England without descending to the ground. Many trees had religious significance and many were believed to have magical properties.

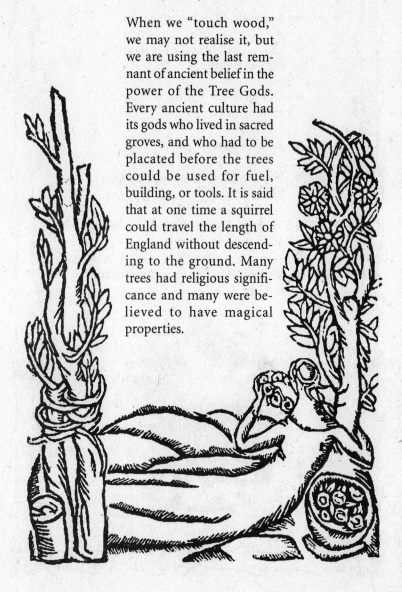

When the Christian religion was introduced things became more complicated, for the tree-worshippers could not take the risk of ignoring the old gods, even while embracing, in the main, the new Deity. Christian beliefs and pagan rites and ceremonies became gradually fused together in a strange mixture of superstitition, faith, and fear of magic. Thus a tree like the elder, for instance, said to be a "witches' tree" and feared, could be used as a magical preventive against evil, and then explained by the belief that its powers were due to the fact that Jesus' cross was made from elder wood. This kind of intermingling of pagan and Christian belief appears over and over again in old legends and stories.

The majestic oak was regarded as a very powerful magic tree, and people believed that the tree would scream and moan if it was cut down. Charms and spells used in divination often involved the oak tree and its acorns.

Hawthorn, too, was a tree of magic powers. Everyone knows the legend of the Holy Thorn at Glastonbury, which blooms on Old Christmas Day. A Holy Thorn would gush real blood if anyone attempted to chop it down. If you sit under a hawthorn in May, the fairies will have power over you. Hawthorn and blackthorn were often burned as firecharms as part of fertility rites. The seeds of hawthorn, boiled in wine, were said by Culpeper to be able to draw out thorns and splinters. Today it is still used as a cardiac tonic, and the young blossoms make a very fine fragrant wine.

The rowan, or mountain ash, is a strong protector against evil. More powerful still was the elder tree, home of the "Old Lady of the Elder," a wicked spirit who waited to gain control over those who loitered beneath the branches.

Furniture made from elder wood would warp and crack, and if used for a baby's cradle, the spirit would attack the child. But it could be used for good purposes too. As a charm, it could identify witches. It keeps flies from the house, and was used to treat snake bite, dog bites, and toothache. It is still used medicinally today, in the form of elderflower lotions and ointments, which are excellent for skin complaints, and bruises and sprains. Both the berries and the flowers make very good country wines.

Lastly, if ever you need to dispose of Dracula, the stake driven through his heart must be made of elder.

Ash was another highly prized tree, and could also repel witches and evil spirits, as well as killing snakes. It was considered to have great curative powers. A lock of the sufferer's hair pinned to the tree would cure whooping cough, and a live mouse or shrew nailed up in a little hole in the bark would cure sheep diseases. To cure toothache, you should sit under an ash tree and cut your toenails.

Ash was also used in love charms and divination, and to find an ash leaf with an even number of "leaflets" was extremely fortunate. An ashen bundle was often burned as a Yule log. Medicinal uses of the ash included poultices of the leaves to cure snake bite, decoction of the leaves to cure jaundice, dropsy, and gout, and the seed kernels for kidney stone and wind.

Holly trees are a good source of domestic protection if you have one in the garden, and yew and hazel were both considered magical trees. Hazel protects from lightning and shipwreck. Cows' milk yield can be increased by giving them hazel leaves to eat. Hazel twigs are used by water diviners even today.

Birch, from which witches' broomsticks were made, was another "magic" tree. Brooms made of birch, or birch twigs in the house, could give protection. But some care was needed, for if an unmarried girl were to step over the birch broom, she would become pregnant. The tars and oils derived from birch are still used in the treatment of eczema and other skin complaints, and a fine wine can be made from the sap, if the tree is tapped in the spring when the sap is rising.

One of the best trees to plant in your garden is the bay tree, which will protect from all kinds of harm, and which is a healthy influence on your home, your family, and pets. It is well known for its culinary uses, and used to have a variety of medicinal uses, including inducing a speedy delivery in childbirth. The berries produced an oil which was good for the joints, the nerves, and the arteries, but now it is only used as a remedy for rheumatism.

Fruit trees and orchards have a wealth of folklore all to themselves. Sacrifices were made to the gods who lived in them, and special fertility rites were carried out to ensure good crops. A last memory of these remains in the apple howling or wassailing ceremonies still carried out in parts of the West Country.

Further back in time, at Christmas, and Twelfth Night, Easter, Beltane, and at Midsummer, great fire festivals were held—a mixture of pagan and Christian beliefs and ceremonies. Their purpose was to save the crops from evil spirits, and to safeguard from hail, lightning, and storms. Fires and feasting also served to welcome back the Sun God at the end of the dark winter, for with his coming the cold Earth would reawaken and bring the renewal of fertility associated with the coming of spring. Powerful magic indeed.

The Snake and the Hunter:
A Teaching Game

You Will Need:

A circle of people
A rattle
One blindfold

Rules:

1. No one may step outside of the circle.
2. The snake is caught when the hunter touches him or her.
3. The hunter may not remove the blindfold until after he or she touches the snake.
4. Circle players may laugh and shout, but they may not tell where the snake is.

To Play:

One person is chosen to be the snake. Another individual is chosen to be the hunter. The remainder of the players stand in a circle around the snake and the hunter. The hunter is blindfolded. The snake must shake the rattle every two seconds and tries to elude the hunter without moving outside of the circle. The game is over when the hunter catches the snake.

Lesson:

The game is not as easy to play as it appears. It is excellent practice to use senses other than your eyes.

Animal Weather Omens

By D.J. Conway

When ants are extremely busy, foul weather is coming.

Bats coming out quickly at sunset and flying in the open air with quick darting movements predict fair and calm weather.

When many bees enter, and none leave the hive, rain will soon come.

When ravens or crows make a sorrowful hollow noise, it predicts the approach of bad weather.

A pig carrying straws in its mouth is a prediction of a coming storm. The Irish say that the pig can see the wind.

In Europe, it is the hedgehog, not the groundhog, who appears on February 2 to fortell the weather.

Almanac Pages
1995 Magical Almanac

Calendar

Time Changes

Full Moon Listings

Sabbat Listings

Lunar Phase Listings

Moon Sign Listings

World Holiday Listings

Color Correspondences

Stone Correspondences

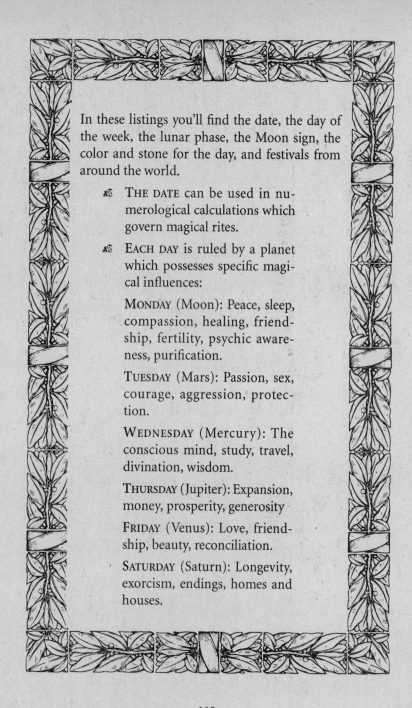

In these listings you'll find the date, the day of the week, the lunar phase, the Moon sign, the color and stone for the day, and festivals from around the world.

- THE DATE can be used in numerological calculations which govern magical rites.

- EACH DAY is ruled by a planet which possesses specific magical influences:

  MONDAY (Moon): Peace, sleep, compassion, healing, friendship, fertility, psychic awareness, purification.

  TUESDAY (Mars): Passion, sex, courage, aggression, protection.

  WEDNESDAY (Mercury): The conscious mind, study, travel, divination, wisdom.

  THURSDAY (Jupiter): Expansion, money, prosperity, generosity

  FRIDAY (Venus): Love, friendship, beauty, reconciliation.

  SATURDAY (Saturn): Longevity, exorcism, endings, homes and houses.

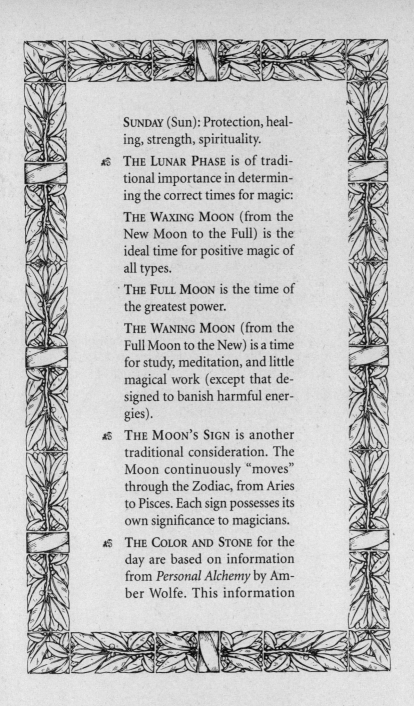

SUNDAY (Sun): Protection, healing, strength, spirituality.

⚡ THE LUNAR PHASE is of traditional importance in determining the correct times for magic:

THE WAXING MOON (from the New Moon to the Full) is the ideal time for positive magic of all types.

THE FULL MOON is the time of the greatest power.

THE WANING MOON (from the Full Moon to the New) is a time for study, meditation, and little magical work (except that designed to banish harmful energies).

⚡ THE MOON'S SIGN is another traditional consideration. The Moon continuously "moves" through the Zodiac, from Aries to Pisces. Each sign possesses its own significance to magicians.

⚡ THE COLOR AND STONE for the day are based on information from *Personal Alchemy* by Amber Wolfe. This information

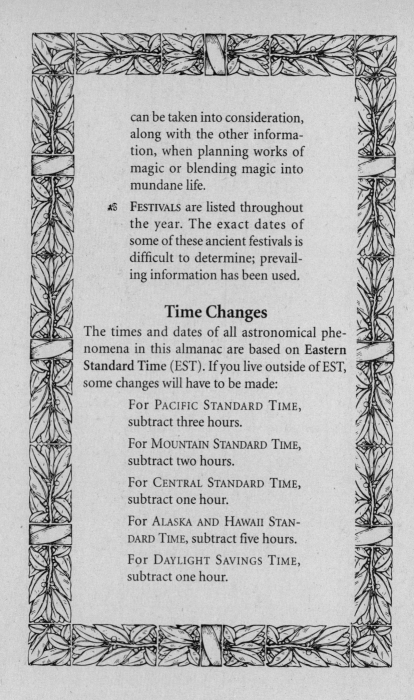

can be taken into consideration, along with the other information, when planning works of magic or blending magic into mundane life.

✿ FESTIVALS are listed throughout the year. The exact dates of some of these ancient festivals is difficult to determine; prevailing information has been used.

Time Changes

The times and dates of all astronomical phenomena in this almanac are based on **Eastern Standard Time (EST)**. If you live outside of EST, some changes will have to be made:

For PACIFIC STANDARD TIME, subtract three hours.

For MOUNTAIN STANDARD TIME, subtract two hours.

For CENTRAL STANDARD TIME, subtract one hour.

For ALASKA AND HAWAII STANDARD TIME, subtract five hours.

For DAYLIGHT SAVINGS TIME, subtract one hour.

1995 Sabbats and Full Moons

January 16	Full Moon 3:27 PM
February 2	Imbolc
February 15	Full Moon 7:16 AM
March 16	Full Moon 8:26 PM
March 20	Ostara (Spring Equinox)
April 15	Full Moon 7:08 AM
May 1	Beltaine
May 14	Full Moon 3:49 PM
June 12	Full Moon 11:04 PM
June 21	Litha (Summer Solstice)
July 12	Full Moon 5:49 PM
August 1	Lammas
August 10	Full Moon 1:16 PM
September 8	Full Moon 10:38 PM
September 23	Mabon (Fall Equinox)
October 8	Full Moon 10:52 AM
October 31	Samhain
November 7	Full Moon 2:20 AM
December 6	Full Moon 8:28 PM
December 22	Yule (Winter Solstice)

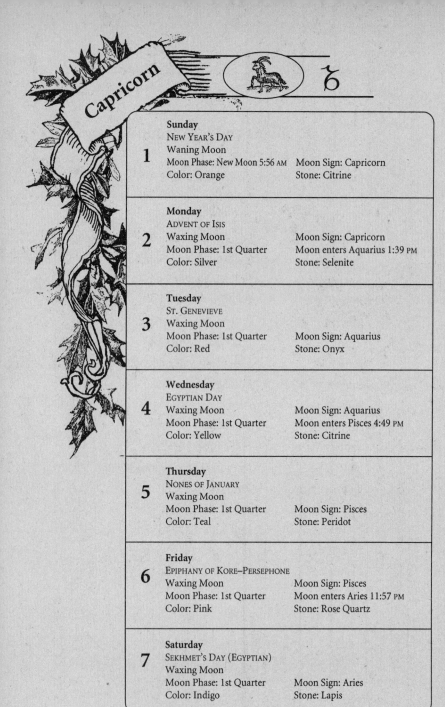

Capricorn ♑

Sunday
NEW YEAR'S DAY
Waning Moon
1 Moon Phase: New Moon 5:56 AM   Moon Sign: Capricorn
Color: Orange   Stone: Citrine

Monday
ADVENT OF ISIS
Waxing Moon   Moon Sign: Capricorn
2 Moon Phase: 1st Quarter   Moon enters Aquarius 1:39 PM
Color: Silver   Stone: Selenite

Tuesday
ST. GENEVIEVE
3 Waxing Moon
Moon Phase: 1st Quarter   Moon Sign: Aquarius
Color: Red   Stone: Onyx

Wednesday
EGYPTIAN DAY
4 Waxing Moon   Moon Sign: Aquarius
Moon Phase: 1st Quarter   Moon enters Pisces 4:49 PM
Color: Yellow   Stone: Citrine

Thursday
NONES OF JANUARY
5 Waxing Moon
Moon Phase: 1st Quarter   Moon Sign: Pisces
Color: Teal   Stone: Peridot

Friday
EPIPHANY OF KORE–PERSEPHONE
6 Waxing Moon   Moon Sign: Pisces
Moon Phase: 1st Quarter   Moon enters Aries 11:57 PM
Color: Pink   Stone: Rose Quartz

Saturday
SEKHMET'S DAY (EGYPTIAN)
7 Waxing Moon
Moon Phase: 1st Quarter   Moon Sign: Aries
Color: Indigo   Stone: Lapis

Sunday
8
JUSTITIA (ROMAN)
Waxing Moon
Moon Phase: 2nd Quarter · Moon Sign: Aries
Color: Gold · Stone: Tiger Eye

Monday
9
FESTIVAL OF JANUS
Waxing Moon · Moon Sign: Aries
Moon Phase: 2nd Quarter · Moon enters Taurus 10:58 AM
Color: Lavender · Stone: Mother of Pearl

Tuesday
10
GERAINT(WELSH)
Waxing Moon
Moon Phase: 2nd Quarter · Moon Sign: Taurus
Color: Gray · Stone: Ruby

Wednesday
11
CARMENTALIA/JUTURNA (ROMAN)
Waxing Moon · Moon Sign: Taurus
Moon Phase: 2nd Quarter · Moon enters Gemini 11:57 PM
Color: White · Stone: Moonstone

Thursday
12
ST. DISTAFF'S DAY
Waxing Moon
Moon Phase: 2nd Quarter · Moon Sign: Gemini
Color: Purple · Stone: Malachite

Friday
13
IDES OF JANUARY
Waxing Moon
Moon Phase: 2nd Quarter · Moon Sign: Gemini
Color: Flax · Stone: Unikite

Saturday
14
MAKAR SANKRATI (HINDU)
Waxing Moon · Moon Sign: Gemini
Moon Phase: 2nd Quarter · Moon enters Cancer 12:20 PM
Color: Brown · Stone: Hematite

Capricorn ♑

Sunday
CARMENTALIA
Waxing Moon
15
Moon Phase: 2nd Quarter   Moon Sign: Cancer
Color: Peach   Stone: Amber

Monday
CONCORDIA
Waxing Moon   Moon Sign: Cancer
16
Moon Phase: Full Moon 3:27 PM   Moon enters Leo 10:37 PM
Color: White   Stone: Hematite

Tuesday
EGYPTIAN DAY
Waning Moon
17
Moon Phase: 3rd Quarter   Moon Sign: Leo
Color: Scarlet   Stone: Obsidian

Wednesday
WOMEN'S FESTIVAL OF JUNO (ROMAN)
Waning Moon
18
Moon Phase: 3rd Quarter   Moon Sign: Leo
Color: Amber   Stone: Tiger Eye

Thursday
FESTIVAL OF THOR (NORSE)
Waning Moon   Moon Sign: Leo
19
Moon Phase: 3rd Quarter   Moon enters Virgo 6:40 AM
Color: Green   Stone: Turquoise

Friday
ST. AGNES' EVE
Waning Moon   Sun enters Aquarius 8:00 AM
20
Moon Phase: 3rd Quarter   Moon Sign: Virgo
Color: Peach   Stone: Abalone

Saturday
CELTIC TREE MONTH OF LUIS BEGINS
Waning Moon   Moon Sign: Virgo
21
Moon Phase: 3rd Quarter   Moon enters Libra 12:54 PM
Color: Blue   Stone: Azurite

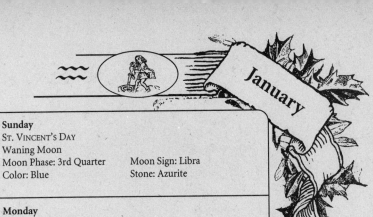

Sunday
ST. VINCENT'S DAY
Waning Moon
Moon Phase: 3rd Quarter   Moon Sign: Libra
Color: Blue   Stone: Azurite

22

Monday
GODDESS MONTH OF BRIDHE BEGINS
Waning Moon   Moon Sign: Libra
Moon Phase: 3rd Quarter   Moon enters Scorpio 5:33 PM
Color: Rust   Stone: Carnelian

23

Tuesday
ST. PAUL'S EVE
Waning Moon
Moon Phase: 4th Quarter   Moon Sign: Scorpio
Color: Purple   Stone: Milky Quartz

24

Wednesday
ST. PAUL'S DAY
Waning Moon   Moon Sign: Scorpio
Moon Phase: 4th Quarter   Moon enters Sagittarius 8:37 PM
Color: Crimson   Stone: Red Jasper

25

Thursday
FEAST OF EKEKO
Waning Moon
Moon Phase: 4th Quarter   Moon Sign: Sagittarius
Color: Brown   Stone: Yellow Jasper

26

Friday
DISTING MOON
Waning Moon   Moon Sign: Sagittarius
Moon Phase: 4th Quarter   Moon enters Capricorn 10:27 PM
Color: Violet   Stone: Amethyst

27

Saturday
RUNIC HALF-MONTH OF ELHAZ BEGINS
Waning Moon
Moon Phase: 4th Quarter   Moon Sign: Capricorn
Color: White   Stone: Opal

28

Aquarius

Sunday
EGYPTIAN DAY

29 Waning Moon
Moon Phase: 4th Quarter   Moon Sign: Capricorn
Color: Yellow   Stone: Fire Agate

Monday
FESTIVAL OF PEACE

30 Waning Moon   Moon Sign: Capricorn
Moon Phase: New Moon 5:48 PM   Moon enters Aquarius 12:03 AM
Color: Silver   Stone: Marble

Tuesday
FEBRUARY EVE

31 Waxing Moon
Moon Phase: 1st Quarter   Moon Sign: Aquarius
Color: Black   Stone: Cinnabar

January Birthstones
Ancient: Garnet
Modern: Garnet

January Flowers
Carnations
Snowdrops

February Birthstones
Ancient: Amethyst
Modern: Amethyst

February Flowers
Violets
Primroses

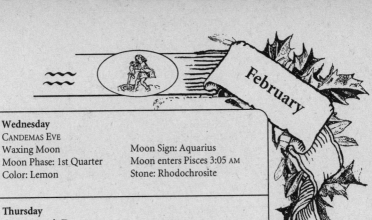

Wednesday

1

CANDEMAS EVE
Waxing Moon
Moon Phase: 1st Quarter
Color: Lemon

Moon Sign: Aquarius
Moon enters Pisces 3:05 AM
Stone: Rhodochrosite

Thursday

2

GROUNDHOG'S DAY
Waxing Moon
Moon Phase: 1st Quarter
Color: Pine

Moon Sign: Pisces
Stone: Tourmaline

Friday

3

ST. BLASIUS
Waxing Moon
Moon Phase: 1st Quarter
Color: Cream

Moon Sign: Pisces
Moon enters Aries 9:12 AM
Stone: Abalone

Saturday

4

KING FROST DAY (ENGLISH)
Waxing Moon
Moon Phase: 1st Quarter
Color: Blue

Moon Sign: Aries
Stone: Azurite

Sunday

5

NONES OF FEBRUARY
Waxing Moon
Moon Phase: 1st Quarter
Color: Pumpkin

Moon Sign: Aries
Moon enters Taurus 7:08 PM
Stone: Fire Agate

Monday

6

ST. DOROTHEA
Waxing Moon
Moon Phase: 1st Quarter
Color: Platinum

Moon Sign: Taurus
Stone: Crystals

Tuesday

7

SELENE'S DAY (GREEK)
Waxing Moon
Moon Phase: 1st Quarter
Color: Charcoal

Moon Sign: Taurus
Stone: Jet–Black Coral

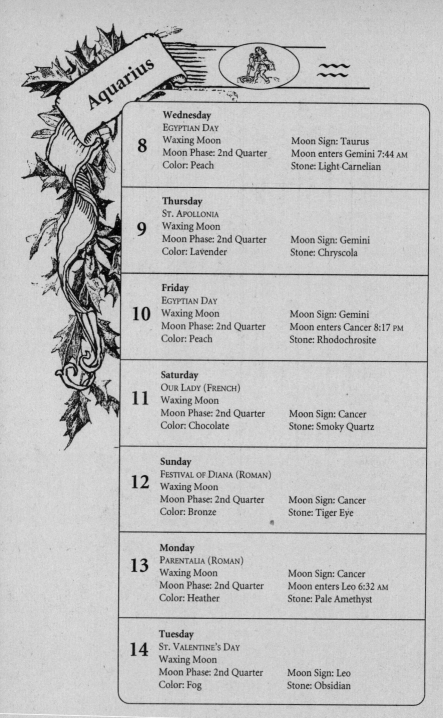

Aquarius

Wednesday
EGYPTIAN DAY
8 Waxing Moon
Moon Phase: 2nd Quarter
Color: Peach

Moon Sign: Taurus
Moon enters Gemini 7:44 AM
Stone: Light Carnelian

Thursday
ST. APOLLONIA
9 Waxing Moon
Moon Phase: 2nd Quarter
Color: Lavender

Moon Sign: Gemini
Stone: Chryscola

Friday
EGYPTIAN DAY
10 Waxing Moon
Moon Phase: 2nd Quarter
Color: Peach

Moon Sign: Gemini
Moon enters Cancer 8:17 PM
Stone: Rhodochrosite

Saturday
OUR LADY (FRENCH)
11 Waxing Moon
Moon Phase: 2nd Quarter
Color: Chocolate

Moon Sign: Cancer
Stone: Smoky Quartz

Sunday
FESTIVAL OF DIANA (ROMAN)
12 Waxing Moon
Moon Phase: 2nd Quarter
Color: Bronze

Moon Sign: Cancer
Stone: Tiger Eye

Monday
PARENTALIA (ROMAN)
13 Waxing Moon
Moon Phase: 2nd Quarter
Color: Heather

Moon Sign: Cancer
Moon enters Leo 6:32 AM
Stone: Pale Amethyst

Tuesday
ST. VALENTINE'S DAY
14 Waxing Moon
Moon Phase: 2nd Quarter
Color: Fog

Moon Sign: Leo
Stone: Obsidian

Wednesday

15

LUPERCALIA (ROMAN)
Waxing Moon
Moon Phase: Full Moon 7:16 AM
Color: White

Moon Sign: Leo
Moon enters Virgo 1:52 AM
Stone: Moonstone

Thursday

16

CELEBRATION OF VICTORIA (ROMAN)
Waning Moon
Moon Phase: 3rd Quarter
Color: Hunter Green

Moon Sign: Virgo
Stone: Aventurine

Friday

17

FORNACALIA (ROMAN)
Waning Moon
Moon Phase: 3rd Quarter
Color: Blush

Moon Sign: Virgo
Moon enters Libra 7:01 PM
Stone: Rose Quartz

Saturday

18

FESTIVAL OF WOMEN (PERSIAN)
Waning Moon
Moon Phase: 3rd Quarter
Color: Gray

Sun enters Pisces 10:11 PM
Moon Sign: Libra
Stone: Lapis

Sunday

19

GODDESS MONTH OF BRIDHE ENDS
Waning Moon
Moon Phase: 3rd Quarter
Color: Orange

Moon Sign: Libra
Moon enters Scorpio 10:55 PM
Stone: Carnelian

Monday

20

GODDESS MONTH OF MOURA BEGINS
Waning Moon
Moon Phase: 3rd Quarter
Color: White

Moon Sign: Scorpio
Stone: Abalone

Tuesday

21

SHIVARATI (HINDU)
Waning Moon
Moon Phase: 3rd Quarter
Color: Red

Moon Sign: Scorpio
Stone: Bloodstone

Pisces

♓

Wednesday
CHARISTIA (ROMAN)
22 Waning Moon
Moon Phase: 4th Quarter
Color: Earth

Moon Sign: Scorpio
Moon enters Sagittarius 2:13 AM
Stone: Amber

Thursday
TERMINALIA (ROMAN)
23 Waning Moon
Moon Phase: 4th Quarter
Color: Violet

Moon Sign: Sagittarius
Stone: Amethyst

Friday
ST. MATTHIAS' DAY
24 Waning Moon
Moon Phase: 4th Quarter
Color: Straw

Moon Sign: Sagittarius
Moon enters Capricorn 5:10 AM
Stone: Opal

Saturday
TIME OF THE OLD WOMAN (MOROCCAN)
25 Waning Moon
Moon Phase: 4th Quarter
Color: Surf

Moon Sign: Capricorn
Stone: Blue Coral

Sunday
EGYPTIAN DAY
26 Waning Moon
Moon Phase: 4th Quarter
Color: Peach

Moon Sign: Capricorn
Moon enters Aquarius 8:14 AM
Stone: Opal

Monday
RUNIC HALF–MONTH OF TYR BEGINS
27 Waning Moon
Moon Phase: 4th Quarter
Color: Violet

Moon Sign: Aquarius
Stone: Fluorite

Tuesday
BUDDHA'S CONCEPTION (TIBETAN)
28 Waning Moon
Moon Phase: 4th Quarter
Color: Ruby

Moon Sign: Aquarius
Moon enters Pisces 12:16 PM
Stone: Apache Tears

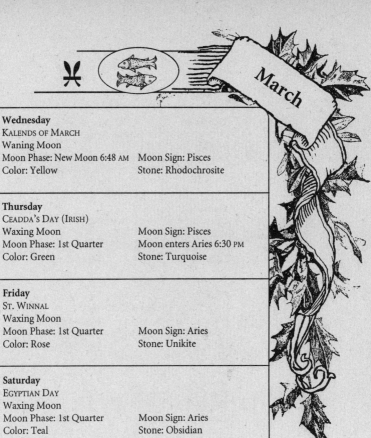

March

Wednesday
KALENDS OF MARCH
Waning Moon
Moon Phase: New Moon 6:48 AM   Moon Sign: Pisces
Color: Yellow   Stone: Rhodochrosite

1

Thursday
CEADDA'S DAY (IRISH)
Waxing Moon
Moon Phase: 1st Quarter   Moon Sign: Pisces
Color: Green   Moon enters Aries 6:30 PM
    Stone: Turquoise

2

Friday
ST. WINNAL
Waxing Moon
Moon Phase: 1st Quarter   Moon Sign: Aries
Color: Rose   Stone: Unikite

3

Saturday
EGYPTIAN DAY
Waxing Moon
Moon Phase: 1st Quarter   Moon Sign: Aries
Color: Teal   Stone: Obsidian

4

Sunday
NAVIGIUM ISIS (EGYPTIAN)
Waxing Moon
Moon Phase: 1st Quarter   Moon Sign: Aries
Color: Gold   Moon enters Taurus 3:51 AM
    Stone: Fire Agate

5

Monday
MARS (ROMAN)
Waxing Moon
Moon Phase: 1st Quarter   Moon Sign: Taurus
Color: Oatmeal   Stone: Milky Quartz

6

Tuesday
PURIM (JEWISH)
Waxing Moon
Moon Phase: 1st Quarter   Moon Sign: Taurus
Color: Crimson   Moon enters Gemini 3:56 PM
    Stone: Hematite

7

Pisces

Wednesday
8
BIRTHDAY OF MOTHER EARTH (CHINESE)
Waxing Moon
Moon Phase: 1st Quarter   Moon Sign: Gemini
Color: Brown   Stone: Tiger Eye

Thursday
9
CELEBRATION OF APHRODITE AND ADONIS (GREEK)
Waxing Moon
Moon Phase: 1st Quarter   Moon Sign: Gemini
Color: Purple   Stone: Aventurine

Friday
10
HOLI (INDIAN SPRING FIRE FESTIVAL)
Waxing Moon   Moon Sign: Gemini
Moon Phase: 2nd Quarter   Moon enters Cancer 4:41 AM
Color: Apricot   Stone: Abalone

Saturday
11
HERAKLES
Waxing Moon
Moon Phase: 2nd Quarter   Moon Sign: Cancer
Color: Brown   Stone: Sodalite

Sunday
12
MARTYRDOM OF HYPATIA
Waxing Moon   Moon Sign: Cancer
Moon Phase: 2nd Quarter   Moon enters Leo 3:29 PM
Color: Orange   Stone: Rutilated Quartz

Monday
13
PURIFICATION FEAST (BALINESE)
Waxing Moon
Moon Phase: 2nd Quarter   Moon Sign: Leo
Color: Platinum   Stone: Silver

Tuesday
14
VETURIUS MAMURIUS
Waxing Moon   Moon Sign: Leo
Moon Phase: 2nd Quarter   Moon enters Virgo 10:55 PM
Color: Ash   Stone: Onyx

March

Wednesday
IDES OF MARCH
15 Waxing Moon
Moon Phase: 2nd Quarter   Moon Sign: Virgo
Color: White   Stone: Light Carnelian

Thursday
FESTIVAL OF DIONYSUS (GREEK)
16 Waxing Moon
Moon Phase: Full Moon 8:26 PM   Moon Sign: Virgo
Color: Pine   Stone: Chryscola

Friday
ST. PATRICK'S DAY (IRISH)
17 Waning Moon   Moon Sign: Virgo
Moon Phase: 3rd Quarter   Moon enters Libra 3:18 AM
Color: White   Stone: Pink Tourmaline

Saturday
ST. EDWARD THE MARTYR (ANGLO–SAXON)
18 Waning Moon
Moon Phase: 3rd Quarter   Moon Sign: Libra
Color: Indigo   Stone: Obsidian

Sunday
EYVIND KINNRIFI (NORSE)
19 Waning Moon   Moon Sign: Libra
Moon Phase: 3rd Quarter   Moon enters Scorpio 5:52 AM
Color: Peach   Stone: Opal

Monday
VERNAL EQUINOX
20 Waning Moon   Sun enters Aries 9:14 PM
Moon Phase: 3rd Quarter   Moon Sign: Scorpio
Color: Violet   Stone: Hematite

Tuesday
TEA AND TEPHI (IRISH)
21 Waning Moon   Moon Sign: Scorpio
Moon Phase: 3rd Quarter   Moon enters Sagittarius 7:57 AM
Color: Red   Stone: Garnet

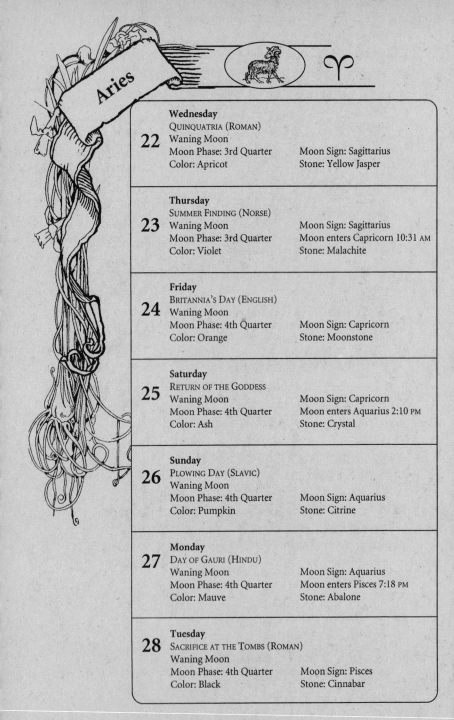

Aries

Wednesday
22
QUINQUATRIA (ROMAN)
Waning Moon
Moon Phase: 3rd Quarter
Color: Apricot

Moon Sign: Sagittarius
Stone: Yellow Jasper

Thursday
23
SUMMER FINDING (NORSE)
Waning Moon
Moon Phase: 3rd Quarter
Color: Violet

Moon Sign: Sagittarius
Moon enters Capricorn 10:31 AM
Stone: Malachite

Friday
24
BRITANNIA'S DAY (ENGLISH)
Waning Moon
Moon Phase: 4th Quarter
Color: Orange

Moon Sign: Capricorn
Stone: Moonstone

Saturday
25
RETURN OF THE GODDESS
Waning Moon
Moon Phase: 4th Quarter
Color: Ash

Moon Sign: Capricorn
Moon enters Aquarius 2:10 PM
Stone: Crystal

Sunday
26
PLOWING DAY (SLAVIC)
Waning Moon
Moon Phase: 4th Quarter
Color: Pumpkin

Moon Sign: Aquarius
Stone: Citrine

Monday
27
DAY OF GAURI (HINDU)
Waning Moon
Moon Phase: 4th Quarter
Color: Mauve

Moon Sign: Aquarius
Moon enters Pisces 7:18 PM
Stone: Abalone

Tuesday
28
SACRIFICE AT THE TOMBS (ROMAN)
Waning Moon
Moon Phase: 4th Quarter
Color: Black

Moon Sign: Pisces
Stone: Cinnabar

Wednesday
St. Mark
29 Waning Moon
Moon Phase: 4th Quarter   Moon Sign: Pisces
Color: Gold   Stone: Citrine

Thursday
Festival of Janus and Concordia
30 Waning Moon   Moon Sign: Pisces
Moon Phase: New Moon 9:09 PM   Moon enters Aries 2:26 AM
Color: Grass   Stone: Amazonite

Friday
Feast of Luna (Roman)
31 Waxing Moon
Moon Phase: 1st Quarter   Moon Sign: Aries
Color: Peach   Stone: Rose Quartz

March Birthstones
Ancient: Jasper
Modern: Bloodstone

March Flowers
Daffodils
Jonquils

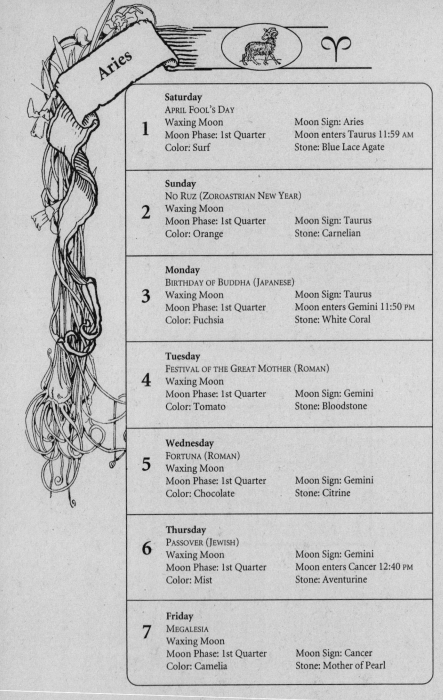

Aries

Saturday

1

April Fool's Day

Waxing Moon

Moon Phase: 1st Quarter

Color: Surf

Moon Sign: Aries

Moon enters Taurus 11:59 AM

Stone: Blue Lace Agate

Sunday

2

No Ruz (Zoroastrian New Year)

Waxing Moon

Moon Phase: 1st Quarter

Color: Orange

Moon Sign: Taurus

Stone: Carnelian

Monday

3

Birthday of Buddha (Japanese)

Waxing Moon

Moon Phase: 1st Quarter

Color: Fuchsia

Moon Sign: Taurus

Moon enters Gemini 11:50 PM

Stone: White Coral

Tuesday

4

Festival of the Great Mother (Roman)

Waxing Moon

Moon Phase: 1st Quarter

Color: Tomato

Moon Sign: Gemini

Stone: Bloodstone

Wednesday

5

Fortuna (Roman)

Waxing Moon

Moon Phase: 1st Quarter

Color: Chocolate

Moon Sign: Gemini

Stone: Citrine

Thursday

6

Passover (Jewish)

Waxing Moon

Moon Phase: 1st Quarter

Color: Mist

Moon Sign: Gemini

Moon enters Cancer 12:40 PM

Stone: Aventurine

Friday

7

Megalesia

Waxing Moon

Moon Phase: 1st Quarter

Color: Camelia

Moon Sign: Cancer

Stone: Mother of Pearl

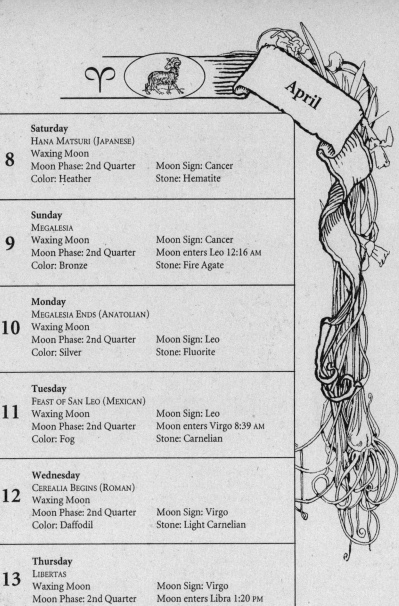

April

Saturday
HANA MATSURI (JAPANESE)
8 Waxing Moon
Moon Phase: 2nd Quarter   Moon Sign: Cancer
Color: Heather   Stone: Hematite

Sunday
MEGALESIA
9 Waxing Moon
Moon Phase: 2nd Quarter   Moon Sign: Cancer
Color: Bronze   Moon enters Leo 12:16 AM
                            Stone: Fire Agate

Monday
MEGALESIA ENDS (ANATOLIAN)
10 Waxing Moon
Moon Phase: 2nd Quarter   Moon Sign: Leo
Color: Silver   Stone: Fluorite

Tuesday
FEAST OF SAN LEO (MEXICAN)
11 Waxing Moon
Moon Phase: 2nd Quarter   Moon Sign: Leo
Color: Fog   Moon enters Virgo 8:39 AM
                            Stone: Carnelian

Wednesday
CEREALIA BEGINS (ROMAN)
12 Waxing Moon
Moon Phase: 2nd Quarter   Moon Sign: Virgo
Color: Daffodil   Stone: Light Carnelian

Thursday
LIBERTAS
13 Waxing Moon
Moon Phase: 2nd Quarter   Moon Sign: Virgo
Color: Violet   Moon enters Libra 1:20 PM
                            Stone: Amethyst

Friday
SOMMARSBLÖT (NORSE)
14 Waxing Moon
Moon Phase: 2nd Quarter   Moon Sign: Libra
Color: Peach   Stone: Moonstone

Aries

Saturday
15
FESTIVAL OF TELLUS (ROMAN)
Waxing Moon
Moon Phase: Full Moon 7:08 AM
Color: Espresso

Moon Sign: Libra
Moon enters Scorpio 3:13 PM
Stone: Smoky Quartz

Sunday
16
ST. PADARN'S DAY (CELTIC)
Waning Moon
Moon Phase: 3rd Quarter
Color: Rust

Moon Sign: Scorpio
Stone: Rutilated Quartz

Monday
17
EGYPTIAN DAY
Waning Moon
Moon Phase: 3rd Quarter
Color: Mauve

Moon Sign: Scorpio
Moon enters Sagittarius 3:52 PM
Stone: Selenite

Tuesday
18
GODDESS MONTH OF MAIA BEGINS
Waning Moon
Moon Phase: 3rd Quarter
Color: Beet

Moon Sign: Sagittarius
Stone: Obsidian

Wednesday
19
CEREALIA (ROMAN)
Waning Moon
Moon Phase: 3rd Quarter
Color: Peach

Moon Sign: Sagittarius
Moon enters Capricorn 4:54 PM
Stone: Yellow Jasper

Thursday
20
EGYPTIAN DAY
Waning Moon
Moon Phase: 3rd Quarter
Color: Clover

Moon Sign: Capricorn
Sun enters Taurus 8:21 AM
Stone: Emerald

Friday
21
DEA ROMA (BUILDING OF ROME BEGINS)
Waning Moon
Moon Phase: 3rd Quarter
Color: White

Moon Sign: Capricorn
Moon enters Aquarius 7:38 PM
Stone: Opal

Saturday
EARTH DAY
Waning Moon
22
Moon Phase: 4th Quarter   Moon Sign: Aquarius
Color: Charcoal   Stone: Hematite

Sunday
ST. GEORGE (ENGLISH)
Waning Moon
23
Moon Phase: 4th Quarter   Moon Sign: Aquarius
Color: Peach   Stone: Opal

Monday
ST. MARK'S EVE
Waning Moon
24
Moon Phase: 4th Quarter   Moon Sign: Aquarius
    Moon enters Pisces 12:51 AM
Color: White   Stone: Pearls

Tuesday
ROBIGALIA (ROMAN)
Waning Moon
25
Moon Phase: 4th Quarter   Moon Sign: Pisces
Color: Black   Stone: Hematite

Wednesday
NEW YEAR'S DAY (SIERRA LEONE)
Waning Moon
26
Moon Phase: 4th Quarter   Moon Sign: Pisces
    Moon enters Aries 8:42 AM
Color: White   Stone: Moonstone

Thursday
FEAST OF ST. GEORGE (BRITISH)
Waning Moon
27
Moon Phase: 4th Quarter   Moon Sign: Aries
Color: Maroon   Stone: Tourmaline

Friday
FLORALIA (ROMAN)
Waning Moon
28
Moon Phase: 4th Quarter   Moon Sign: Aries
    Moon enters Taurus 6:53 PM
Color: Rose   Stone: Rainbow Quartz

Taurus

Saturday

29 RUNIC HALF-MONTH OF LAGU BEGINS
Waning Moon
Moon Phase: New Moon 12:37 PM   Moon Sign: Taurus
Color: Gray   Stone: Sodalite

Sunday

30 WALPURGISNACHT (GERMAN)
Waxing Moon
Moon Phase: 1st Quarter   Moon Sign: Taurus
Color: Tangerine   Stone: Rhodochrosite

April Birthstones
Ancient: Sapphire
Modern: Diamond

April Flowers
Daisies
Sweet Peas

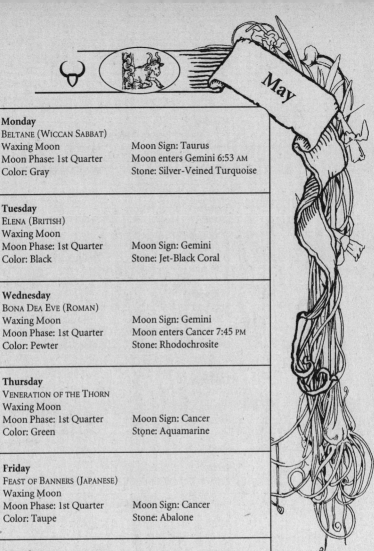

May

Monday

1

BELTANE (WICCAN SABBAT)
Waxing Moon
Moon Phase: 1st Quarter
Color: Gray

Moon Sign: Taurus
Moon enters Gemini 6:53 AM
Stone: Silver-Veined Turquoise

Tuesday

2

ELENA (BRITISH)
Waxing Moon
Moon Phase: 1st Quarter
Color: Black

Moon Sign: Gemini
Stone: Jet-Black Coral

Wednesday

3

BONA DEA EVE (ROMAN)
Waxing Moon
Moon Phase: 1st Quarter
Color: Pewter

Moon Sign: Gemini
Moon enters Cancer 7:45 PM
Stone: Rhodochrosite

Thursday

4

VENERATION OF THE THORN
Waxing Moon
Moon Phase: 1st Quarter
Color: Green

Moon Sign: Cancer
Stone: Aquamarine

Friday

5

FEAST OF BANNERS (JAPANESE)
Waxing Moon
Moon Phase: 1st Quarter
Color: Taupe

Moon Sign: Cancer
Stone: Abalone

Saturday

6

ENLIGHTENMENT OF THE BUDDHA
Waxing Moon
Moon Phase: 1st Quarter
Color: Indigo

Moon Sign: Cancer
Moon enters Leo 7:55 AM
Stone: Blue Tiger Eye

Sunday

7

HELSTON FURRY DANCE (WELSH)
Waxing Moon
Moon Phase: 2nd Quarter
Color: Tangerine

Moon Sign: Leo
Stone: Amber

Monday
BIRTHDAY OF JULIAN OF NORWICH
8
Waxing Moon
Moon Phase: 2nd Quarter
Color: White

Moon Sign: Leo
Moon enters Virgo 5:33 PM
Stone: Marble

Tuesday
LEMURIA (ROMAN)
9
Waxing Moon
Moon Phase: 2nd Quarter
Color: Gray

Moon Sign: Virgo
Stone: Apache Tears

Wednesday
FESTIVAL: TIN HAU'S DAY (CHINESE)
10
Waxing Moon
Moon Phase: 2nd Quarter
Color: Lemon

Moon Sign: Virgo
Moon enters Libra 11:30 PM
Stone: Citrine

Thursday
ST. MAMERTIUS (GERMAN)
11
Waxing Moon
Moon Phase: 2nd Quarter
Color: Purple

Moon Sign: Libra
Stone: Malachite

Friday
FESTIVAL OF SASHTI (INDIAN)
12
Waxing Moon
Moon Phase: 2nd Quarter
Color: Rose

Moon Sign: Libra
Stone: Pink Tourmaline

Saturday
GARLAND DAY (ENGLISH)
13
Waxing Moon
Moon Phase: 2nd Quarter
Color: Mauve

Moon Sign: Libra
Moon enters Scorpio 1:54 AM
Stone: Lapis

Sunday
GODDESS OF TITHE FESTIVAL (NORTH AFRICAN)
14
Waxing Moon
Moon Phase: Full Moon 3:49 PM
Color: Peach

Moon Sign: Scorpio
Stone: Rhodochrosite

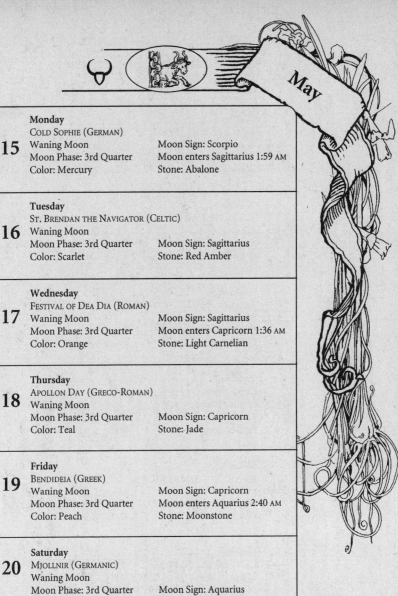

Monday
15 COLD SOPHIE (GERMAN)
Waning Moon
Moon Phase: 3rd Quarter
Color: Mercury

Moon Sign: Scorpio
Moon enters Sagittarius 1:59 AM
Stone: Abalone

Tuesday
16 ST. BRENDAN THE NAVIGATOR (CELTIC)
Waning Moon
Moon Phase: 3rd Quarter
Color: Scarlet

Moon Sign: Sagittarius
Stone: Red Amber

Wednesday
17 FESTIVAL OF DEA DIA (ROMAN)
Waning Moon
Moon Phase: 3rd Quarter
Color: Orange

Moon Sign: Sagittarius
Moon enters Capricorn 1:36 AM
Stone: Light Carnelian

Thursday
18 APOLLON DAY (GRECO-ROMAN)
Waning Moon
Moon Phase: 3rd Quarter
Color: Teal

Moon Sign: Capricorn
Stone: Jade

Friday
19 BENDIDEIA (GREEK)
Waning Moon
Moon Phase: 3rd Quarter
Color: Peach

Moon Sign: Capricorn
Moon enters Aquarius 2:40 AM
Stone: Moonstone

Saturday
20 MJOLLNIR (GERMANIC)
Waning Moon
Moon Phase: 3rd Quarter
Color: Surf

Moon Sign: Aquarius
Stone: Sodalite

Sunday
21 PLATO'S BIRTHDAY
Waning Moon
Moon Phase: 4th Quarter
Color: Mango

Moon Sign: Aquarius
Moon enters Pisces 6:40 AM
Sun enters Gemini 7:34 AM
Stone: Fire Agate

Monday
RAGNAR LODBROK (NORSE)
22 Waning Moon
Moon Phase: 4th Quarter   Moon Sign: Pisces
Color: Cream   Stone: White Agate

Tuesday
ROSALIA (ROMAN)
23 Waning Moon   Moon Sign: Pisces
Moon Phase: 4th Quarter   Moon enters Aries 2:13 PM
Color: Navy   Stone: Granite

Wednesday
TRIPLE GODDESS DAY (CELTIC)
24 Waning Moon
Moon Phase: 4th Quarter   Moon Sign: Aries
Color: Lemon   Stone: Yellow Fluorite

Thursday
ENLIGHTENMENT OF BUDDHA
25 Waning Moon
Moon Phase: 4th Quarter   Moon Sign: Aries
Color: Mauve   Stone: Amazonite

Friday
DAY OF CHIN-HUA-FU-JEN (CHINESE)
26 Waning Moon   Moon Sign: Aries
Moon Phase: 4th Quarter   Moon enters Taurus 12:46 AM
Color: Bone   Stone: Mother of Pearl

Saturday
CENTENNIAL GAMES (ROMAN)
27 Waning Moon
Moon Phase: 4th Quarter   Moon Sign: Taurus
Color: Straw   Stone: Azurite

Sunday
FEAST OF THE DEAD (BUDDHIST)
28 Waning Moon   Moon Sign: Taurus
Moon Phase: 4th Quarter   Moon enters Gemini 1:07 PM
Color: Gold   Stone: Opal

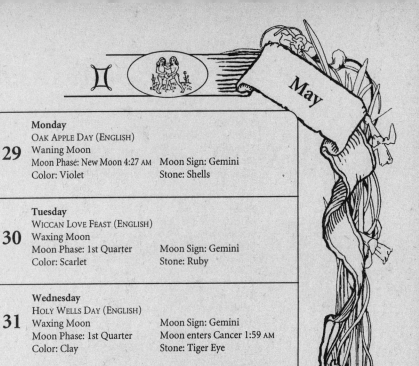

Monday

29

OAK APPLE DAY (ENGLISH)
Waning Moon
Moon Phase: New Moon 4:27 AM   Moon Sign: Gemini
Color: Violet   Stone: Shells

Tuesday

30

WICCAN LOVE FEAST (ENGLISH)
Waxing Moon
Moon Phase: 1st Quarter   Moon Sign: Gemini
Color: Scarlet   Stone: Ruby

Wednesday

31

HOLY WELLS DAY (ENGLISH)
Waxing Moon
Moon Phase: 1st Quarter   Moon Sign: Gemini
Color: Clay   Moon enters Cancer 1:59 AM
                          Stone: Tiger Eye

May Birthstones
Ancient: Agate
Modern: Emerald

May Flowers
Lilies of the Valley
Hawthorn

Gemini

1
Thursday
FESTIVAL OF SYN (NORSE)
Waxing Moon
Moon Phase: 1st Quarter — Moon Sign: Cancer
Color: Grass — Stone: Green Quartz

2
Friday
MOTHER SHIPTON'S DAY (ENGLISH)
Waxing Moon — Moon Sign: Cancer
Moon Phase: 1st Quarter — Moon enters Leo 2:17 PM
Color: Pink — Stone: Moonstone

3
Saturday
BROKEN DOLLS DAY (JAPANESE)
Waxing Moon
Moon Phase: 1st Quarter — Moon Sign: Leo
Color: Marine Blue — Stone: Sapphire

4
Sunday
BIRTHDAY OF SOCRATES
Waxing Moon
Moon Phase: 1st Quarter — Moon Sign: Leo
Color: Yellow — Stone: Carnelian

5
Monday
ST. GOBNATT (IRISH)
Waxing Moon — Moon Sign: Leo
Moon Phase: 1st Quarter — Moon enters Virgo 12:47 AM
Color: Sand — Stone: Selenite

6
Tuesday
NIGHT OF OBSERVATION (MOSLEM)
Waxing Moon
Moon Phase: 1st Quarter — Moon Sign: Virgo
Color: Pomegranate — Stone: Cinnabar

7
Wednesday
VESTALIA (ROMAN)
Waxing Moon — Moon Sign: Virgo
Moon Phase: 2nd Quarter — Moon enters Libra 8:14 AM
Color: Daffodil — Stone: Yellow Fluorite

Thursday

8

LINDISFARNE DAY (NORSE)
Waxing Moon
Moon Phase: 2nd Quarter
Color: Magenta

Moon Sign: Libra
Stone: Chryscola

Friday

9

VESTIA (ROMAN)
Waxing Moon
Moon Phase: 2nd Quarter
Color: White

Moon Sign: Libra
Moon enters Scorpio 12:04 PM
Stone: Unikite

Saturday

10

DAY OF ANAHITA (PERSIAN)
Waxing Moon
Moon Phase: 2nd Quarter
Color: Black

Moon Sign: Scorpio
Stone: Petrified Wood

Sunday

11

DAY OF FORTUNA (ROME)
Waxing Moon
Moon Phase: 2nd Quarter
Color: Bronze

Moon Sign: Scorpio
Moon enters Sagittarius 12:50 PM
Stone: Rutilated Quartz

Monday

12

FEAST OF MUT (EGYPTIAN)
Waxing Moon
Moon Phase: Full Moon 11:04 PM
Color: Pewter

Moon Sign: Sagittarius
Stone: White Coral

Tuesday

13

TIBETAN ALL SAINTS' DAY
Waning Moon
Moon Phase: 3rd Quarter
Color: Gray

Moon Sign: Sagittarius
Moon enters Capricorn 12:05 PM
Stone: Red Jasper

Wednesday

14

VIDAR'S DAY (NORSE)
Waning Moon
Moon Phase: 3rd Quarter
Color: White

Moon Sign: Capricorn
Stone: Citrine

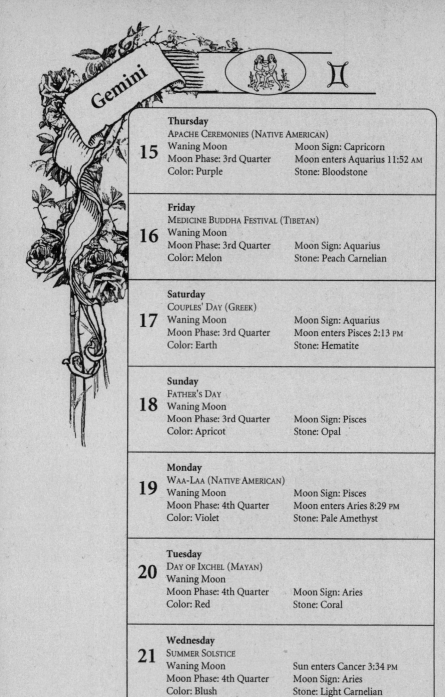

Gemini

15 **Thursday**
APACHE CEREMONIES (NATIVE AMERICAN)
Waning Moon
Moon Phase: 3rd Quarter
Color: Purple

Moon Sign: Capricorn
Moon enters Aquarius 11:52 AM
Stone: Bloodstone

16 **Friday**
MEDICINE BUDDHA FESTIVAL (TIBETAN)
Waning Moon
Moon Phase: 3rd Quarter
Color: Melon

Moon Sign: Aquarius
Stone: Peach Carnelian

17 **Saturday**
COUPLES' DAY (GREEK)
Waning Moon
Moon Phase: 3rd Quarter
Color: Earth

Moon Sign: Aquarius
Moon enters Pisces 2:13 PM
Stone: Hematite

18 **Sunday**
FATHER'S DAY
Waning Moon
Moon Phase: 3rd Quarter
Color: Apricot

Moon Sign: Pisces
Stone: Opal

19 **Monday**
WAA-LAA (NATIVE AMERICAN)
Waning Moon
Moon Phase: 4th Quarter
Color: Violet

Moon Sign: Pisces
Moon enters Aries 8:29 PM
Stone: Pale Amethyst

20 **Tuesday**
DAY OF IXCHEL (MAYAN)
Waning Moon
Moon Phase: 4th Quarter
Color: Red

Moon Sign: Aries
Stone: Coral

21 **Wednesday**
SUMMER SOLSTICE
Waning Moon
Moon Phase: 4th Quarter
Color: Blush

Sun enters Cancer 3:34 PM
Moon Sign: Aries
Stone: Light Carnelian

June

Thursday
22 CANDELARIA FOR YEMAYA (BRAZILIAN)
Waning Moon
Moon Phase: 4th Quarter
Color: Khaki

Moon Sign: Aries
Moon enters Taurus 6:35 AM
Stone: Malachite

Friday
23 DAY OF CUCHULAINE (IRISH)
Waning Moon
Moon Phase: 4th Quarter
Color: Straw

Moon Sign: Taurus
Stone: Abalone

Saturday
24 AZTEC FEAST OF THE SUN
Waning Moon
Moon Phase: 4th Quarter
Color: Indigo

Moon Sign: Taurus
Moon enters Gemini 7:02 PM
Stone: Obsidian

Sunday
25 TARTAR FESTIVAL OF THE PLOW
Waning Moon
Moon Phase: 4th Quarter
Color: Goldenrod

Moon Sign: Gemini
Stone: Fire Agate

Monday
26 Waning Moon
Moon Phase: 4th Quarter
Color: White

Moon Sign: Gemini
Stone: Moonstone

Tuesday
27 FESTIVAL OF JULIAN THE BLESSED (ROMAN)
Waning Moon
Moon Phase: New Moon 7:51 PM
Color: Black

Moon Sign: Gemini
Moon enters Cancer 7:57 AM
Stone: Marble

Wednesday
28 BIRTHDAY OF HEMERA (GREEK)
Waxing Moon
Moon Phase: 1st Quarter
Color: Peach

Moon Sign: Cancer
Stone: Amber

Cancer ♋

Thursday
RUNIC NEW YEAR
29 Waxing Moon
Moon Phase: 1st Quarter
Color: Pine

Moon Sign: Cancer
Moon enters Leo 8:02 PM
Stone: Emerald

Friday
AESTAS' DAY (CORN GODDESS)
30 Waxing Moon
Moon Phase: 1st Quarter
Color: Rose

Moon Sign: Leo
Stone: Rainbow Quartz

June Birthstones
Ancient: Emerald
Modern: Agate

June Flowers
Roses
Honeysuckle

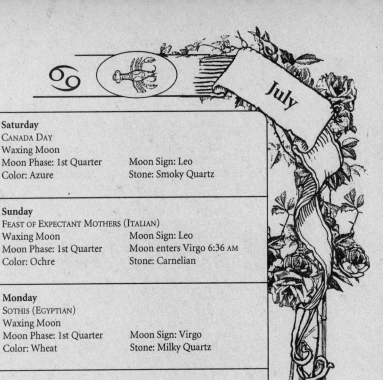

July

Saturday

1

CANADA DAY
Waxing Moon
Moon Phase: 1st Quarter
Color: Azure

Moon Sign: Leo
Stone: Smoky Quartz

Sunday

2

FEAST OF EXPECTANT MOTHERS (ITALIAN)
Waxing Moon
Moon Phase: 1st Quarter
Color: Ochre

Moon Sign: Leo
Moon enters Virgo 6:36 AM
Stone: Carnelian

Monday

3

SOTHIS (EGYPTIAN)
Waxing Moon
Moon Phase: 1st Quarter
Color: Wheat

Moon Sign: Virgo
Stone: Milky Quartz

Tuesday

4

INDEPENDENCE DAY
Waxing Moon
Moon Phase: 1st Quarter
Color: Persimmon

Moon Sign: Virgo
Moon enters Libra 2:56 PM
Stone: Carnelian

Wednesday

5

SUN DANCE FESTIVAL (NATIVE AMERICAN)
Waxing Moon
Moon Phase: 2nd Quarter
Color: Yellow

Moon Sign: Libra
Stone: Citrine

Thursday

6

RUNNING OF THE BULLS (SPANISH)
Waxing Moon
Moon Phase: 2nd Quarter
Color: Purple

Moon Sign: Libra
Moon enters Scorpio 8:19 PM
Stone: Aventurine

Friday

7

FESTIVAL OF CONSUALIA (ROMAN)
Waxing Moon
Moon Phase: 2nd Quarter
Color: Rose

Moon Sign: Scorpio
Stone: Rainbow Quartz

Cancer

♋

Saturday
FEAST OF ST. SUNNIVA
8
Waxing Moon
Moon Phase: 2nd Quarter
Color: Brown

Moon Sign: Scorpio
Moon enters Sagittarius 10:38 PM
Stone: Obsidian

Sunday
LOBSTER CARNIVAL (NOVA SCOTIA)
9
Waxing Moon
Moon Phase: 2nd Quarter
Color: Gold

Moon Sign: Sagittarius
Stone: Amber

Monday
LADY GODIVA DAY (ENGLISH)
10
Waxing Moon
Moon Phase: 2nd Quarter
Color: Violet

Moon Sign: Sagittarius
Moon enters Capricorn 10:43 PM
Stone: Amethyst

Tuesday
THEANO'S DAY (PATRONESS OF VEGETARIANISM)
11
Waxing Moon
Moon Phase: 2nd Quarter
Color: Charcoal

Moon Sign: Capricorn
Stone: Onyx

Wednesday
OLD DANCES (BUDDHIST)
12
Waxing Moon
Moon Phase: Full Moon 5:49 AM
Color: Taupe

Moon Sign: Capricorn
Moon enters Aquarius 10:21 PM
Stone: Rhodochrosite

Thursday
REED DANCE DAY (AFRICAN)
13
Waning Moon
Moon Phase: 3rd Quarter
Color: Green

Moon Sign: Aquarius
Stone: Peridot

Friday
BASTILLE DAY (FRENCH)
14
Waning Moon
Moon Phase: 3rd Quarter
Color: Bone

Moon Sign: Aquarius
Moon enters Pisces 11:37 PM
Stone: Moonstone

July

Saturday
15
DAY OF RAUNI (FINNISH)
Waning Moon
Moon Phase: 3rd Quarter   Moon Sign: Pisces
Color: Rust   Stone: Sodalite

Sunday
16
BIRTHDAY OF SET (EGYPTIAN)
Waning Moon
Moon Phase: 3rd Quarter   Moon Sign: Pisces
Color: Tangerine   Stone: Rhodochrosite

Monday
17
FESTIVAL OF AMATERASU (JAPANESE SUN GODDESS)
Waning Moon   Moon Sign: Pisces
Moon Phase: 3rd Quarter Moon enters Aries 4:23 AM
Color: Silver   Stone: Selenite

Tuesday
18
BIRTHDAY OF NEPTHYS (EGYPTIAN)
Waning Moon
Moon Phase: 3rd Quarter   Moon Sign: Aries
Color: Crimson   Stone: Garnet

Wednesday
19
EGYPTIAN NEW YEAR
Waning Moon   Moon Sign: Aries
Moon Phase: 4th Quarter Moon enters Taurus 1:21 PM
Color: Citron   Stone: Light Carnelian

Thursday
20
BINDING OF THE WREATHS (LITHUANIAN)
Waning Moon
Moon Phase: 4th Quarter   Moon Sign: Taurus
Color: Plum   Stone: Bloodstone

Friday
21
MAYAN NEW YEAR
Waning Moon
Moon Phase: 4th Quarter   Moon Sign: Taurus
Color: Rose   Stone: Rhodochrosite

Leo ♌

Saturday
CHOCTAW FESTIVAL (NATIVE AMERICAN)
22
Waning Moon   Moon Sign: Taurus
Moon Phase: 4th Quarter   Moon enters Gemini 1:24 AM
Color: Navy   Stone: Lapis

Sunday
NEPTUNALIA (ROMAN)
23
Waning Moon   Sun enters Leo 2:30 AM
Moon Phase: 4th Quarter   Moon Sign: Gemini
Color: Yellow   Stone: Fire Agate

Monday
24
Waning Moon   Moon Sign: Gemini
Moon Phase: 4th Quarter   Moon enters Cancer 2:17 PM
Color: White   Stone: Crystals

Tuesday
NAGA PANCHAMI (INDIAN)
25
Waning Moon
Moon Phase: 4th Quarter   Moon Sign: Cancer
Color: Black   Stone: Cinnabar

Wednesday
PUEBLO BUFFALO AND CORN DANCES (NATIVE AMERICAN)
26
Waning Moon
Moon Phase: 4th Quarter   Moon Sign: Cancer
Color: Peach   Stone: Yellow Jasper

Thursday
ST. PANTALEONE'S DAY (PATRON SAINT OF TROUSERS)
27
Waning Moon   Moon Sign: Cancer
Moon Phase: New Moon 10:14 AM Moon enters Leo 2:07 AM
Color: Clover   Stone: Green Fluorite

Friday
START OF GATHERING TIME (CELTIC)
28
Waxing Moon
Moon Phase: 1st Quarter   Moon Sign: Leo
Color: Sand   Stone: Opal

Saturday

FEAST OF SANTA MARTA (MEXICAN)

29
Waxing Moon
Moon Phase: 1st Quarter
Color: Charcoal

Moon Sign: Leo
Moon enters Virgo 12:13 PM
Stone: Hematite

Sunday

MICMAC FESTIVAL OF ST. ANN

30
Waxing Moon
Moon Phase: 1st Quarter
Color: Apricot

Moon Sign: Virgo
Stone: Citrine

Monday

OIDCHE LUGNASA (CELTIC)

31
Waxing Moon
Moon Phase: 1st Quarter
Color: Magenta

Moon Sign: Virgo
Moon enters Libra 8:24 PM
Stone: Abalone

July Birthstones
Ancient: Onyx
Modern: Ruby

July Flowers
Water Lilies
Larkspur

Leo ♌

Tuesday
LAMMAS (WICCAN SABBAT)
Waxing Moon
Moon Phase: 1st Quarter   Moon Sign: Libra
Color: Pomegranate   Stone: Red Amber

1

Wednesday
FEAST OF OUR LADY OF ANGELS (COSTA RICAN BLACK MADONNA)
Waxing Moon
Moon Phase: 1st Quarter   Moon Sign: Libra
Color: Peach   Stone: Yellow Jasper

2

Thursday
Waxing Moon   Moon Sign: Libra
Moon Phase: 2nd Quarter   Moon enters Scorpio 2:29 AM
Color: Ivy   Stone: Green Quartz

3

Friday
VIGIL OF ST. OSWALD (ANGLO-SAXON)
Waxing Moon
Moon Phase: 2nd Quarter   Moon Sign: Scorpio
Color: Pink   Stone: Rhodochrosite

4

Saturday
SHOSHONE-BANNOCK BEGINS (NATIVE AMERICAN)
Waxing Moon   Moon Sign: Scorpio
Moon Phase: 2nd Quarter   Moon enters Sagittarius 6:14 AM
Color: Clove   Stone: Crystals

5

Sunday
FESTIVAL OF THOTH (EGYPTIAN)
Waxing Moon
Moon Phase: 2nd Quarter   Moon Sign: Sagittarius
Color: Flame   Stone: Carnelian

6

Monday
BREAKING OF THE NILE (EGYPTIAN)
Waxing Moon   Moon Sign: Sagittarius
Moon Phase: 2nd Quarter   Moon enters Capricorn 7:52 AM
Color: Lava   Stone: Milky Quartz

7

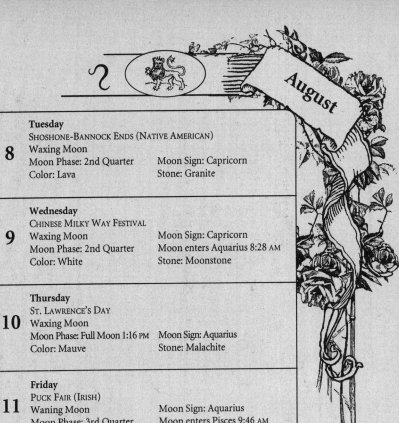

August

Tuesday
8
SHOSHONE-BANNOCK ENDS (NATIVE AMERICAN)
Waxing Moon
Moon Phase: 2nd Quarter   Moon Sign: Capricorn
Color: Lava   Stone: Granite

Wednesday
9
CHINESE MILKY WAY FESTIVAL
Waxing Moon
Moon Phase: 2nd Quarter   Moon Sign: Capricorn
Color: White   Moon enters Aquarius 8:28 AM
                                 Stone: Moonstone

Thursday
10
ST. LAWRENCE'S DAY
Waxing Moon
Moon Phase: Full Moon 1:16 PM   Moon Sign: Aquarius
Color: Mauve   Stone: Malachite

Friday
11
PUCK FAIR (IRISH)
Waning Moon
Moon Phase: 3rd Quarter   Moon Sign: Aquarius
Color: Cream   Moon enters Pisces 9:46 AM
                                 Stone: Abalone

Saturday
12
GRAPE FESTIVAL (ARMENIAN)
Waning Moon
Moon Phase: 3rd Quarter   Moon Sign: Pisces
Color: Blue   Stone: Sodalite

Sunday
13
FESTIVAL OF DIANA (ROMAN)
Waning Moon
Moon Phase: 3rd Quarter   Moon Sign: Pisces
Color: Gold   Moon enters Aries 1:41 PM
                                 Stone: Amber

Monday
14
Waning Moon
Moon Phase: 3rd Quarter   Moon Sign: Aries
Color: Platinum   Stone: Moonstone

Leo ♌

Tuesday
15
MOON FESTIVAL (CHINESE)
Waning Moon
Moon Phase: 3rd Quarter
Color: Vermilion

Moon Sign: Aries
Moon enters Taurus 9:26 PM
Stone: Coral

Wednesday
16
FESTIVAL OF MINSTRELS (EUROPEAN)
Waning Moon
Moon Phase: 3rd Quarter
Color: Daffodil

Moon Sign: Taurus
Stone: Citrine

Thursday
17
ODIN'S ORDEAL BEGINS (NORSE)
Waning Moon
Moon Phase: 3rd Quarter
Color: Golden-Green

Moon Sign: Taurus
Stone: Emerald

Friday
18
ST. HELENA'S DAY
Waning Moon
Moon Phase: 4th Quarter
Color: Melon

Moon Sign: Taurus
Moon enters Gemini 8:40 AM
Stone: Rose Quartz

Saturday
19
RUSTIC VINALIA (ROMAN)
Waning Moon
Moon Phase: 4th Quarter
Color: Cinnamon

Moon Sign: Gemini
Stone: Obsidian

Sunday
20
HOPI FLUTE CEREMONY
Waning Moon
Moon Phase: 4th Quarter
Color: Yellow

Moon Sign: Gemini
Moon enters Cancer 9:24 PM
Stone: Fire Agate

Monday
21
HERACLIA IN KYNOSARGES (GREEK)
Waning Moon
Moon Phase: 4th Quarter
Color: Oatmeal

Moon Sign: Cancer
Stone: White Coral

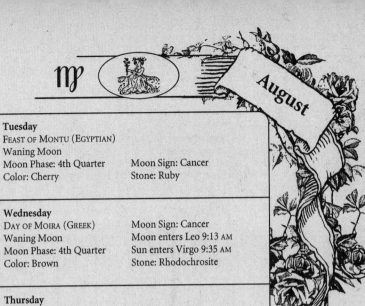

Tuesday
22 FEAST OF MONTU (EGYPTIAN)
Waning Moon
Moon Phase: 4th Quarter   Moon Sign: Cancer
Color: Cherry   Stone: Ruby

Wednesday
23 DAY OF MOIRA (GREEK)
Waning Moon   Moon Sign: Cancer
Moon Phase: 4th Quarter   Moon enters Leo 9:13 AM
Color: Brown   Sun enters Virgo 9:35 AM
                               Stone: Rhodochrosite

Thursday
24 ST. BARTHOLOMEW'S DAY
Waning Moon
Moon Phase: 4th Quarter   Moon Sign: Leo
Color: Lavender   Stone: Chryscola

Friday
25 ODIN'S ORDEAL ENDS
Waning Moon   Moon Sign: Leo
Moon Phase: New Moon 11:31 PM Moon enters Virgo 6:50 PM
Color: Geranium   Stone: Opal

Saturday
26 FEAST DAY OF ILMATAR (FINNISH)
Waxing Moon
Moon Phase: 1st Quarter   Moon Sign: Virgo
Color: Black   Stone: Blue Tiger Eye

Sunday
27 WORSHIP OF GODDESS DEVAKI (EAST INDIAN)
Waxing Moon
Moon Phase: 1st Quarter   Moon Sign: Virgo
Color: Clay   Stone: Opal

Monday
28 NORSE HARVEST FESTIVAL
Waxing Moon   Moon Sign: Virgo
Moon Phase: 1st Quarter   Moon enters Libra 2:15 AM
Color: Royal Purple   Stone: Hematite

Tuesday
ST. ROSE OF LIMA DAY (PERUVIAN)

29
PARDON OF THE SEA (BRITTANY)
Waxing Moon
Moon Phase: 1st Quarter   Moon Sign: Libra
Color: Black   Stone: Apache Tears

Wednesday
ST. ROSE OF LIMA DAY (PERUVIAN)

30
Waxing Moon   Moon Sign: Libra
Moon Phase: 1st Quarter   Moon enters Scorpio 7:51 AM
Color: Lemon   Stone: Tiger Eye

Thursday
Waxing Moon

31
Moon Phase: 1st Quarter   Moon Sign: Scorpio
Color: Fuchsia   Stone: Amazonite

August Birthstones
Ancient: Carnelian
Modern: Topaz

August Flowers
Gladiolus
Poppies

Friday
St. Giles' Day (Patron Saint of the Disabled)

1
Waxing Moon
Moon Phase: 1st Quarter
Color: Papaya

Moon Sign: Scorpio
Moon enters Sagittarius 11:57 AM
Stone: Pink Tourmaline

Saturday
Feast of Asar Unnefer (Egyptian)

2
Waxing Moon
Moon Phase: 2nd Quarter
Color: Coffee

Moon Sign: Sagittarius
Stone: Fluorite

Sunday
La Kon (Hopi)

3
Waxing Moon
Moon Phase: 2nd Quarter
Color: Copper

Moon Sign: Sagittarius
Moon enters Capricorn 2:45 PM
Stone: Carnelian

Monday
Labor Day

4
Waxing Moon
Moon Phase: 2nd Quarter
Color: Oyster

Moon Sign: Capricorn
Stone: Mother of Pearl

Tuesday
Day of Nanda Devi (East Indian)

5
Waxing Moon
Moon Phase: 2nd Quarter
Color: Ochre

Moon Sign: Capricorn
Moon enters Aquarius 4:48 PM
Stone: Garnet

Wednesday
Goddess Month of Mala Begins

6
Waxing Moon
Moon Phase: 2nd Quarter
Color: Apricot

Moon Sign: Aquarius
Stone: Amber

Thursday
Festival of Durga (Bengalese)

7
Waxing Moon
Moon Phase: 2nd Quarter
Color: Palm

Moon Sign: Aquarius
Moon enters Pisces 7:09 PM
Stone: Green Fluorite

Friday
PINNHUT FESTIVAL (NATIVE AMERICAN)
8 Waxing Moon
Moon Phase: Full Moon 10:38 PM   Moon Sign: Pisces
Color: Straw   Stone: Unikite

Saturday
HORNED DANCE (ENGLISH)
9 Waning Moon   Moon Sign: Pisces
Moon Phase: 3rd Quarter   Moon enters Aries 11:15 PM
Color: Black   Stone: Petrified Wood

Sunday
EGYPTIAN DAY OF QUEENS
10 Waning Moon
Moon Phase: 3rd Quarter   Moon Sign: Aries
Color: Peach   Stone: Citrine

Monday
FAST OF GADALYA (JEWISH)
11 Waning Moon
Moon Phase: 3rd Quarter   Moon Sign: Aries
Color: Silver   Stone: Hematite

Tuesday
THIRD GAHAMBAR (ZOROASTRIAN)
12 Waning Moon   Moon Sign: Aries
Moon Phase: 3rd Quarter   Moon enters Taurus 6:22 AM
Color: Crimson   Stone: Red Jasper

Wednesday
LIGHTING THE FIRE (EGYPTIAN)
13 Waning Moon
Moon Phase: 3rd Quarter   Moon Sign: Taurus
Color: Clove   Stone: Rhodochrosite

Thursday
HOLY ROOD DAY
14 Waning Moon   Moon Sign: Taurus
Moon Phase: 3rd Quarter   Moon enters Gemini 4:48 PM
Color: Orchid   Stone: Malachite

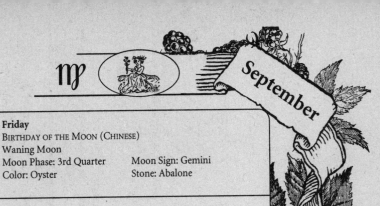

Friday
BIRTHDAY OF THE MOON (CHINESE)
Waning Moon
15
Moon Phase: 3rd Quarter   Moon Sign: Gemini
Color: Oyster   Stone: Abalone

Saturday
ST. NINIAN'S DAY
Waning Moon
16
Moon Phase: 3rd Quarter   Moon Sign: Gemini
Color: Boysenberry   Stone: Blue Coral

Sunday
FESTIVAL OF SABEK (EGYPTIAN)
Waning Moon   Moon Sign: Gemini
17
Moon Phase: 4th Quarter   Moon enters Cancer 5:16 AM
Color: Orange   Stone: Rhodochrosite

Monday
EGYPTIAN DAY
Waning Moon
18
Moon Phase: 4th Quarter   Moon Sign: Cancer
Color: Freesia   Stone: Pale Amethyst

Tuesday
DAY OF GULA (BABYLONIAN)
Waning Moon   Moon Sign: Cancer
19
Moon Phase: 4th Quarter   Moon enters Leo 5:19 PM
Color: Gray   Stone: Fire Agate

Wednesday
BIRTHDAY OF QUETZACOATL (INCAN)
Waning Moon
20
Moon Phase: 4th Quarter   Moon Sign: Leo
Color: Bronze   Stone: Light Carnelian

Thursday
RAUDTHESTRONG (NORSE)
Waning Moon
21
Moon Phase: 4th Quarter   Moon Sign: Leo
Color: Pine   Stone: Tourmaline

Libra

Friday
22
DAY OF MIELIKKI (FINNISH)
Waning Moon
Moon Phase: 4th Quarter
Color: Mango

Moon Sign: Leo
Moon enters Virgo 3:01 AM
Stone: Peach Carnelian

Saturday
23
MABON (WICCAN SABBAT)
Waning Moon
Moon Phase: 4th Quarter
Color: Indigo

Moon Sign: Virgo
Sun enters Libra 7:13 AM
Stone: Lapis

Sunday
24
Waning Moon
Moon Phase: New Moon 11:55 AM
Color: Rust

Moon Sign: Virgo
Moon enters Libra 9:50 AM
Stone: Fire Agate

Monday
25
ROSH HASHANAH (JEWISH)
Waxing Moon
Moon Phase: 1st Quarter
Color: Silver

Moon Sign: Libra
Stone: Selenite

Tuesday
26
DIVALI (INDIAN)
Waxing Moon
Moon Phase: 1st Quarter
Color: Carmine

Moon Sign: Libra
Moon enters Scorpio 2:20 PM
Stone: Coral

Wednesday
27
DAY OF WILLOWS (MESOPOTAMIAN)
Waxing Moon
Moon Phase: 1st Quarter
Color: Flax

Moon Sign: Scorpio
Stone: Citrine

Thursday
28
FEAST OF ZISA
Waxing Moon
Moon Phase: 1st Quarter
Color: Fuchsia

Moon enters Sagittarius 5:31 PM
Moon Sign: Scorpio
Stone: Amethyst

Friday

FEAST OF NEMESIS (GREEK)

29 Waxing Moon

Moon Phase: 1st Quarter   Moon Sign: Sagittarius

Color: Rose   Stone: Opal

Saturday

MEDETRINALIA (ROMAN)

30 Waxing Moon

Moon Phase: 1st Quarter   Moon Sign: Sagittarius

Color: Taupe   Moon enters Capricorn 8:11 PM

                          Stone: Obsidian

September Birthstones

Ancient: Chrysolite

Modern: Beryl

September Flowers

Morning Glories

Asters

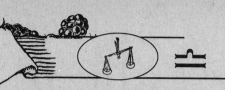

Libra

Sunday
FESTIVAL OF FIDES (ROMAN)
Waxing Moon
Moon Phase: 2nd Quarter
Color: Sienna

1

Moon Sign: Capricorn
Stone: Rhodochrosite

Monday
FEAST OF THE GUARDIAN SPIRITS (DRUIDIC)
Waxing Moon
Moon Phase: 2nd Quarter
Color: Platinum

2

Moon Sign: Capricorn
Moon enters Aquarius 11:00 PM
Stone: Mother of Pearl

Tuesday
MOROCCAN NEW YEAR
Waxing Moon
Moon Phase: 2nd Quarter
Color: Lava

3

Moon Sign: Aquarius
Stone: Coral

Wednesday
YOM KIPPUR (JEWISH)
Waxing Moon
Moon Phase: 2nd Quarter
Color: Banana

4

Moon Sign: Aquarius
Stone: Tiger Eye

Thursday
DAY OF THE HOLY SPIRIT (GNOSTIC)
Waxing Moon
Moon Phase: 2nd Quarter
Color: Green

5

Moon Sign: Aquarius
Moon enters Pisces 2:36 AM
Stone: Aventurine

Friday
FEAST OF ZAPOPAN VIRGIN (MEXICAN)
Waxing Moon
Moon Phase: 2nd Quarter
Color: Peach

6

Moon Sign: Pisces
Stone: Moonstone

Saturday
FEAST OF SHU (EGYPTIAN)
Waxing Moon
Moon Phase: 2nd Quarter
Color: Iron

7

Moon Sign: Pisces
Moon enters Aries 7:42 AM
Stone: Sodalite

October

Sunday
8
START OF FADING TIME (CELTIC)
Waxing Moon
Moon Phase: Full Moon 10:52 AM   Moon Sign: Aries
Color: Copper   Stone: Citrine

Monday
9
COLUMBUS' DAY/SUCCOTH
Waning Moon   Moon Sign: Aries
Moon Phase: 3rd Quarter   Moon enters Taurus 3:05 PM
Color: Fuchsia   Stone: Rainbow Quartz

Tuesday
10
INOKO (JAPANESE)
Waning Moon
Moon Phase: 3rd Quarter   Moon Sign: Taurus
Color: Red   Stone: Obsidian

Wednesday
11
VINALIA (ROMAN WINE TASTING FESTIVAL)
Waning Moon
Moon Phase: 3rd Quarter   Moon Sign: Taurus
Color: Bark   Stone: Rhodochrosite

Thursday
12
FOURTH GAHAMBAR (ZOROASTRIAN)
Waning Moon   Moon Sign: Taurus
Moon Phase: 3rd Quarter   Moon enters Gemini 1:10 AM
Color: Mauve   Stone: Jade

Friday
13
FLOATING OF THE LAMPS (SIAMESE)
Waning Moon
Moon Phase: 3rd Quarter   Moon Sign: Gemini
Color: Oyster   Stone: Pink Tourmaline

Saturday
14
DURGA PUJA (INDIAN)
Waning Moon   Moon Sign: Gemini
Moon Phase: 3rd Quarter   Moon enters Cancer 1:20 PM
Color: Teal   Stone: Blue Coral

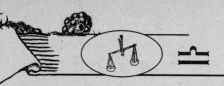

Libra

Sunday
NORSE NEW YEAR
15 Waning Moon
Moon Phase: 3rd Quarter   Moon Sign: Cancer
Color: Cinnamon   Stone: Amber

Monday
CERA FESTIVAL (IRISH)
16 Waning Moon
Moon Phase: 4th Quarter   Moon Sign: Cancer
Color: White   Stone: Marble

Tuesday
FESTIVAL OF DEPARTED WORTHIES (TIBETAN)
17 Waning Moon   Moon Sign: Cancer
Moon Phase: 4th Quarter   Moon enters Leo 1:47 AM
Color: Black   Stone: Red Jasper

Wednesday
FESTIVAL OF HERNE (CELTIC)
18 Waning Moon
Moon Phase: 4th Quarter   Moon Sign: Leo
Color: Peach   Stone: Yellow Jasper

Thursday
BETTARA (JAPANESE)
19 Waning Moon   Moon Sign: Leo
Moon Phase: 4th Quarter   Moon enters Virgo 12:12 PM
Color: Indigo   Stone: Green Fluorite

Friday
FESTIVAL OF ANCESTORS (CHINESE)
20 Waning Moon
Moon Phase: 4th Quarter   Moon Sign: Virgo
Color: Hemp   Stone: Opal

Saturday
KOUREOTIS (GREEK)
21 Waning Moon   Moon Sign: Virgo
Moon Phase: 4th Quarter   Moon enters Libra 7:16 PM
Color: Teal   Stone: Smoky Quartz

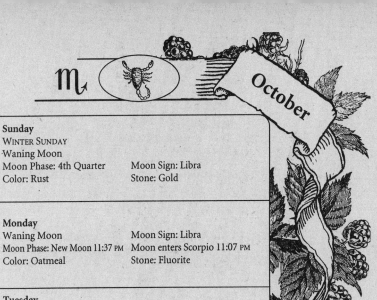

Sunday
22
WINTER SUNDAY
Waning Moon
Moon Phase: 4th Quarter
Color: Rust

Moon Sign: Libra
Stone: Gold

Monday
23
Waning Moon
Moon Phase: New Moon 11:37 PM
Color: Oatmeal

Moon Sign: Libra
Moon enters Scorpio 11:07 PM
Stone: Fluorite

Tuesday
24
UNITED NATIONS DAY
Waxing Moon
Moon Phase: 1st Quarter
Color: Tomato

Moon Sign: Scorpio
Sun enters Scorpio 4:31 PM
Stone: Ruby

Wednesday
25
CRISPIN'S FEAST (ROMAN)
Waxing Moon
Moon Phase: 1st Quarter
Color: Sienna

Moon Sign: Scorpio
Stone: Light Carnelian

Thursday
26
ABAN JASPAN (JAPANESE)
Waxing Moon
Moon Phase: 1st Quarter
Color: Violet

Moon Sign: Scorpio
Moon enters Sagittarius 12:57 AM
Stone: Bloodstone

Friday
27
OWAGLT (HOPI)
Waxing Moon
Moon Phase: 1st Quarter
Color: Nectarine

Moon Sign: Sagittarius
Stone: Rose Quartz

Saturday
28
NORSE FYRIBOD FESTIVAL
Waxing Moon
Moon Phase: 1st Quarter
Color: Navy

Moon Sign: Sagittarius
Moon enters Capricorn 2:15 AM
Stone: Blue Tiger Eye

Scorpio ♏

29	**Sunday** Feast of the Dead (Iroquois) Waxing Moon Moon Phase: 1st Quarter Color: Apricot	Moon Sign: Capricorn Stone: Rutilated Quartz	

Sunday
Feast of the Dead (Iroquois)
29 Waxing Moon
Moon Phase: 1st Quarter Moon Sign: Capricorn
Color: Apricot Stone: Rutilated Quartz

Monday
Angelitos (Mexican)
30 Waxing Moon Moon Sign: Capricorn
Moon Phase: k1st Quarter Moon enters Aquarius 4:24 AM
Color: Lavender Stone: Pale Amethyst

Tuesday
Samhain (Wiccan Sabbat)
31 Waxing Moon
Moon Phase: 2nd Quarter Moon Sign: Aquarius
Color: Steel Stone: Onyx

October Birthstones
Ancient: Aquamarine
Modern: Pearl

October Flowers
Calendula
Cosmos

Wednesday
ALL SAINTS' DAY

1
Waxing Moon
Moon Phase: 2nd Quarter   Moon Sign: Aquarius
Color: Gold   Moon enters Pisces 8:18 AM
Stone: Amber

Thursday
ANIMAS (MEXICAN)

2
Waxing Moon
Moon Phase: 2nd Quarter   Moon Sign: Pisces
Color: Green   Stone: Jade

Friday
NEW YEAR FESTIVAL (GAELIC)

3
Waxing Moon   Moon Sign: Pisces
Moon Phase: 2nd Quarter   Moon enters Aries 2:21 PM
Color: Melon   Stone: Moonstone

Saturday
ST. HUMBERT'S MASS (BELGIAN)

4
Waxing Moon
Moon Phase: 2nd Quarter   Moon Sign: Aries
Color: Marine Blue   Stone: Sapphire

Sunday
WUWUCHIM FIRE CEREMONY (HOPI)

5
Waxing Moon   Moon Sign: Aries
Moon Phase: 2nd Quarter   Moon enters Taurus 10:35 PM
Color: Bronze   Stone: Carnelian

Monday
BIRTHDAY OF TIAMAT (BABYLONIAN)

6
Waxing Moon
Moon Phase: 2nd Quarter   Moon Sign: Taurus
Color: White   Stone: Silver-Veined Turquoise

Tuesday
MAKAHIKI HARVEST FESTIVAL (HAWAIIAN)

7
Waxing Moon
Moon Phase: Full Moon 2:20 AM   Moon Sign: Taurus
Color: Ebony   Stone: Cinnabar

Scorpio ♏

Wednesday
FESTIVAL FOR THE HEARTH (JAPANESE)

8
Waning Moon
Moon Phase: 3rd Quarter
Color: Clove

Moon Sign: Taurus
Moon enters Gemini 8:55 AM
Stone: Citrine

Thursday
FEAST OF LIGHTS (THAI)

9
Waning Moon
Moon Phase: 3rd Quarter
Color: Purple

Moon Sign: Gemini
Stone: Amazonite

Friday
GODDESS OF REASON (FRENCH)

10
Waning Moon
Moon Phase: 3rd Quarter
Color: Bone

Moon Sign: Gemini
Moon enters Cancer 8:57 PM
Stone: Pink Tourmaline

Saturday
GURU NAMAK'S BIRTHDAY (SIKH)

11
Waning Moon
Moon Phase: 3rd Quarter
Color: Coffee

Moon Sign: Cancer
Stone: Fluorite

Sunday
BIRTHDAY OF BAHA'U'LLAH (FOUNDER OF THE BAHA'I FAITH)

12
Waning Moon
Moon Phase: 3rd Quarter
Color: Papaya

Moon Sign: Cancer
Stone: Rhodochrosite

Monday
FESTIVAL OF JUPITER (ROME)

13
Waning Moon
Moon Phase: 3rd Quarter
Color: Lavender

Moon Sign: Cancer
Moon enters Leo 9:38 AM
Stone: Selenite

Tuesday
FEAST OF THE MUSICIANS (DRUIDIC)

14
Waning Moon
Moon Phase: 3rd Quarter
Color: Scarlet

Moon Sign: Leo
Stone: Obsidian

Wednesday
DAY OF FERONA (ITALIAN)
15 Waning Moon   Moon Sign: Leo
Moon Phase: 4th Quarter   Moon enters Virgo 9:03 PM
Color: Cream   Stone: Yellow Fluorite

Thursday
NIGHT OF HECATE (GREEK)
16 Waning Moon
Moon Phase: 4th Quarter   Moon Sign: Virgo
Color: Ivy   Stone: Amethyst

Friday
FEAST OF ST. HILDA
17 Waning Moon
Moon Phase: 4th Quarter   Moon Sign: Virgo
Color: Peach   Stone: Opal

Saturday
DAY OF MOTHER OF STARS (PERSIAN)
18 Waning Moon   Moon Sign: Virgo
Moon Phase: 4th Quarter   Moon enters Libra 5:18 AM
Color: Black   Stone: Black Lace Agate

Sunday
BHARATRI DWITYA (HINDU)
19 Waning Moon
Moon Phase: 4th Quarter   Moon Sign: Libra
Color: Gold   Stone: Tiger Eye

Monday
REVOLUTION DAY (MEXICAN)
20 Waning Moon   Moon Sign: Libra
Moon Phase: 4th Quarter   Moon enters Scorpio 9:41 AM
Color: Silver   Stone: Pearls

Tuesday
DAY OF KULKUKAN (MAYAN)
21 Waning Moon
Moon Phase: 4th Quarter   Moon Sign: Scorpio
Color: Pomegranate   Stone: Red Amber

Sagittarius

Wednesday
22
NORSE WINTER FESTIVAL
Waning Moon
Moon Phase: New Moon 10:43 AM
Color: Earth

Moon Sign: Scorpio
Moon enters Sagittarius 10:57 AM
Sun enters Sagittarius 2:01 PM
Stone: Tiger Eye

Thursday
23
THANKSGIVING DAY
Waxing Moon
Moon Phase: 1st Quarter
Color: Blueberry

Moon Sign: Sagittarius
Stone: Malachite

Friday
24
FEAST OF BURNING LAMPS (EGYPTIAN)
Waxing Moon
Moon Phase: 1st Quarter
Color: Pink

Moon Sign: Sagittarius
Moon enters Capricorn 10:48 AM
Stone: Rainbow Quartz

Saturday
25
FEAST OF GAIA (GREEK)
Waxing Moon
Moon Phase: 1st Quarter
Color: Teal

Moon Sign: Capricorn
Stone: Hematite

Sunday
26
FESTIVAL OF LIGHTS (TIBETAN)
Waxing Moon
Moon Phase: 1st Quarter
Color: Orange

Moon Sign: Capricorn
Moon enters Aquarius 11:15 AM
Stone: Carnelian

Monday
27
GODDESS MONTH OF CAILLEACH ENDS
Waxing Moon
Moon Phase: 1st Quarter
Color: Orchid

Moon Sign: Aquarius
Stone: Marble

Tuesday
28
DAY OF SOPHIA (GREEK)
Waxing Moon
Moon Phase: 1st Quarter
Color: Charcoal

Moon Sign: Aquarius
Moon enters Pisces 1:59 PM
Stone: Coral

Wednesday

DAY OF MAWU (AFRICAN)

29 Waxing Moon

Moon Phase: 2nd Quarter   Moon Sign: Pisces

Color: Peach   Stone: Rhodochrosite

Thursday

ST. ANDREW'S DAY

30 Waxing Moon   Moon Sign: Pisces

Moon Phase: 2nd Quarter   Moon enters Aries 7: 51 PM

Color: Pine   Stone: Green Quartz

November Birthstones
Ancient: Topaz
Modern: Topaz

November Flowers
Chrysanthemums
Dahlias

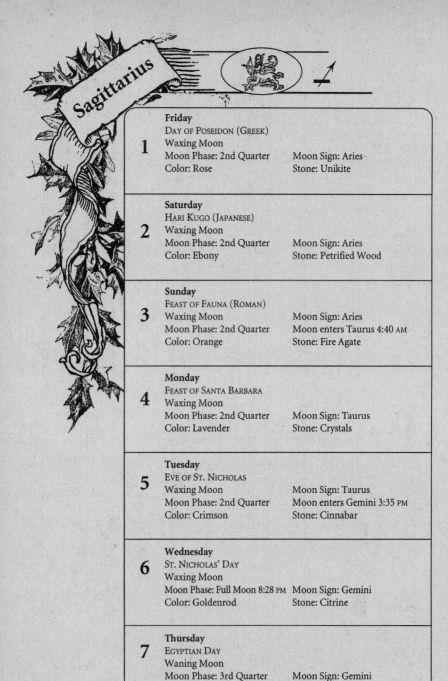

Sagittarius

1
Friday
DAY OF POSEIDON (GREEK)
Waxing Moon
Moon Phase: 2nd Quarter   Moon Sign: Aries
Color: Rose   Stone: Unikite

2
Saturday
HARI KUGO (JAPANESE)
Waxing Moon
Moon Phase: 2nd Quarter   Moon Sign: Aries
Color: Ebony   Stone: Petrified Wood

3
Sunday
FEAST OF FAUNA (ROMAN)
Waxing Moon   Moon Sign: Aries
Moon Phase: 2nd Quarter   Moon enters Taurus 4:40 AM
Color: Orange   Stone: Fire Agate

4
Monday
FEAST OF SANTA BARBARA
Waxing Moon
Moon Phase: 2nd Quarter   Moon Sign: Taurus
Color: Lavender   Stone: Crystals

5
Tuesday
EVE OF ST. NICHOLAS
Waxing Moon   Moon Sign: Taurus
Moon Phase: 2nd Quarter   Moon enters Gemini 3:35 PM
Color: Crimson   Stone: Cinnabar

6
Wednesday
ST. NICHOLAS' DAY
Waxing Moon
Moon Phase: Full Moon 8:28 PM   Moon Sign: Gemini
Color: Goldenrod   Stone: Citrine

7
Thursday
EGYPTIAN DAY
Waning Moon
Moon Phase: 3rd Quarter   Moon Sign: Gemini
Color: Sage   Stone: Emerald

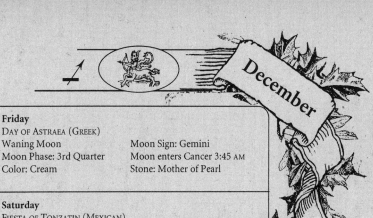

Friday
DAY OF ASTRAEA (GREEK)

8 Waning Moon   Moon Sign: Gemini
Moon Phase: 3rd Quarter   Moon enters Cancer 3:45 AM
Color: Cream   Stone: Mother of Pearl

Saturday
FIESTA OF TONZATIN (MEXICAN)

9 Waning Moon
Moon Phase: 3rd Quarter   Moon Sign: Cancer
Color: Indigo   Stone: Smoky Quartz

Sunday
GODDESS OF LIBERTY DAY (FRENCH)

10 Waning Moon   Moon Sign: Cancer
Moon Phase: 3rd Quarter   Moon enters Leo 4:25 PM
Color: Persimmon   Stone: Amber

Monday
DAY OF BRUMA (ROMAN)

11 Waning Moon
Moon Phase: 3rd Quarter   Moon Sign: Leo
Color: Royal Purple   Stone: Hematite

Tuesday
DAY OF COATLICUE (AZTEC)

12 Waning Moon
Moon Phase: 3rd Quarter   Moon Sign: Leo
Color: Red   Stone: Onyx

Wednesday
HOPI WINTER CEREMONY

13 Waning Moon   Moon Sign: Leo
Moon Phase: 3rd Quarter   Moon enters Virgo 4:27 AM
Color: Espresso   Stone: Light Carnelian

Thursday
FESTIVAL OF NOSTRADAMUS (FRENCH)

14 Waning Moon
Moon Phase: 3rd Quarter   Moon Sign: Virgo
Color: Pine   Stone: Peridot

Friday
15 HALCYON DAYS BEGIN (GREEK)
Waning Moon   Moon Sign: Virgo
Moon Phase: 4th Quarter   Moon enters Libra 2:09 PM
Color: Rose   Stone: Rainbow Quartz

Saturday
16 FESTIVAL OF SAPIENTIA (ROMAN)
Waning Moon
Moon Phase: 4th Quarter   Moon Sign: Libra
Color: Navy   Stone: Hematite

Sunday
17 POSADAS (MEXICAN)
Waning Moon   Moon Sign: Libra
Moon Phase: 4th Quarter   Moon enters Scorpio 8:07 PM
Color: Daffodil   Stone: Rhodochrosite

Monday
18 HANUKKAH (JEWISH)
Waning Moon
Moon Phase: 4th Quarter   Moon Sign: Scorpio
Color: Flax   Stone: White Agate

Tuesday
19 HINDU SOLSTICE
Waning Moon   Moon Sign: Scorpio
Moon Phase: 4th Quarter   Moon enters Sagittarius 10:13 PM
Color: Rust   Stone: Carnelian

Wednesday
20 THE MOTHER NIGHT (ODINIST)
Waning Moon
Moon Phase: 4th Quarter   Moon Sign: Sagittarius
Color: White   Stone: Creamy Moonstone

Thursday
21 YULE (WICCAN SABBAT)
Waning Moon   Moon Sign: Sagittarius
Moon Phase: New Moon 9:22 PM   Moon enters Capricorn 9:46 PM
Color: Violet   Stone: Tourmaline

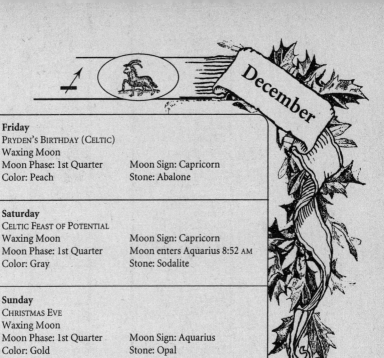

December

Friday
22
PRYDEN'S BIRTHDAY (CELTIC)
Waxing Moon
Moon Phase: 1st Quarter
Color: Peach

Moon Sign: Capricorn
Stone: Abalone

Saturday
23
CELTIC FEAST OF POTENTIAL
Waxing Moon
Moon Phase: 1st Quarter
Color: Gray

Moon Sign: Capricorn
Moon enters Aquarius 8:52 AM
Stone: Sodalite

Sunday
24
CHRISTMAS EVE
Waxing Moon
Moon Phase: 1st Quarter
Color: Gold

Moon Sign: Aquarius
Stone: Opal

Monday
25
CHRISTMAS DAY
Waxing Moon
Moon Phase: 1st Quarter
Color: Pewter

Moon Sign: Aquarius
Moon enters Pisces 9:45 PM
Stone: Crystals

Tuesday
26
BOXING DAY (ENGLISH)
Waxing Moon
Moon Phase: 1st Quarter
Color: Scarlet

Moon Sign: Pisces
Stone: Red Amber

Wednesday
27
RETURN OF KACHINAS (HOPI/PUEBLO)
Waxing Moon
Moon Phase: 1st Quarter
Color: Sand

Moon Sign: Pisces
Stone: Citrine

Thursday
28
BAIRN'S DAY (CELTIC)
Waxing Moon
Moon Phase: 2nd Quarter
Color: Pine Green

Moon Sign: Pisces
Moon enters Aries 2:06 AM
Stone: Emerald

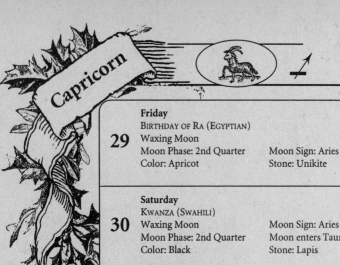

Capricorn

Friday
29
BIRTHDAY OF RA (EGYPTIAN)
Waxing Moon
Moon Phase: 2nd Quarter   Moon Sign: Aries
Color: Apricot   Stone: Unikite

Saturday
30
KWANZA (SWAHILI)
Waxing Moon   Moon Sign: Aries
Moon Phase: 2nd Quarter   Moon enters Taurus 10:22 AM
Color: Black   Stone: Lapis

Sunday
31
NEW YEAR'S EVE
Waxing Moon
Moon Phase: 2nd Quarter   Moon Sign: Taurus
Color: Pumpkin   Stone: Amber

December Birthstones
Ancient: Ruby
Modern: Bloodstone

December Flowers
Narcissus
Holly

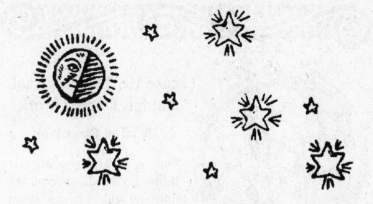

June 25: The Feast of the Hunter's Moon

By Edain McCoy

The Hunter's Moon has its roots in the old folk practices of Eastern Europe. It was originally a night to honor the Goddess and God of the hunt. On the Full Moon nearest the Summer Solstice, summer game animals were hunted with the aid of the Full Moon's light and communal feasts were held to celebrate the bounty of the hunt. A portion of the harvest was sacrificed to the Lady of the Hunt and her consort, the Stag God.

Excuse Me, This Magickal Thingie Doesn't Work

By Silver RavenWolf

During a Tarot reading last winter, my female client turned to me and said, "I have a dream catcher hanging in my daughter's bedroom. I love it and so does she, but it doesn't work." She stuck out her lower lip and sighed. "I also have a hex sign for prosperity I picked up in Lancaster last fall. It doesn't work either."

We chatted for awhile, and I realized that neither my client, nor her sister, were magickally inclined. The sister saw the idea for a dream catcher in a craft magazine and thought that simply by making it, the legends around the item would come true. The client fancied the stories of hex signs, stopped at a tourist trap, and picked up a fairly large one. Neither item felt the touch of a magickal person. In both these instances the buyer assumed the legends around the items were all that was needed in order to make them "go." Wrong.

You don't have to be an expert occultist to tap into ancestral magick that births a legend. Since my client was not involved in magick at all, I gave her this formula:

"Take the dream catcher down and make a pentacle over it in the air. (I showed her how and explained that the pentacle was a very old symbol of protection and banishment.) The five points stand for earth, air, fire, water, and the spirit of man. The circle represents the spirit of the Universe.

At this point she asked me, "Can I use the symbol of the cross?"

"No. Originally, the cross stood for attack. You don't want that on your dream catcher. If you like the idea of a cross, however, use an equal armed one. That will work just as well."

She was satisfied with this answer. My client was a non-practicing Christian.

"Now, you and your daughter hold the dream catcher between you and pray. Ask that the positive energy of God instill the object with love and pleasant dreams. Visualize white light pulsating around and in the dream catcher. Don't be surprised if you can actually see it glow. Children have a knack for doing that. When you are finished, you and your daughter can thank God together and hang the dream catcher up."

If you do have magickal training, choose the proper phase of the moon, the correct planetary hour and day. Do all your work in a magick circle. During the empowerment process, concentrate on the use of the item, as well as the legend that surrounds it. No matter what your belief system, you can make that hex sign, statue, symbol, or dream catcher work for you.

Practical Magick in a Pinch

By Silver RavenWolf

Pow-Wow magick, still practiced in the south central area of Pennsylvania, provides simple remedies that not only work, but pack a mighty wallop. Whenyou don't have the time for intricate workings, try some of these.

Have trouble with nose bleeds?

Empower a red ribbon to tie around your neck.

Bad dreams?

Empower three crushed cloves of garlic. Put them under your bed.

Somebody bothering you?

Take their picture and nail it to a fence post.

Thief ran off with something?

Hang a mirror in your house facing the front door.

Gossip running rampant?

Tie a red piece of yarn around a horse chestnut. Hang it from the highest point in your home.

Need to break a fever fast?

Rub your pillow with lavender.

Bad energy coming your way?

Take your shirt off, turn it inside out, and pinch it in your dresser drawer till morning.

Romantic Rosemary

By Mary Brown

Rosemary, that favorite cottage garden bush, has magical and holy associations reaching back many centuries. It was believed to protect against witchcraft, injury, lightning, and evil spirits. Many superstitions have grown up around its cultivation and use, including its efficacy as a hair restorer, for it was said that if you used a comb made of rosemary wood you would never go bald. A box made from the wood, if smelled daily, would ensure eternal youth. A spoon made from rosemary wood could carry no poison to the lips, and a sprig placed under the bed would make sure the occupant had no bad dreams. Girls used charms containing rosemary and other herbs to find out who their future husbands might be.

Rosemary had connections, too, with the Virgin Mary. It was said that the flowers were originally white, but that the Virgin Mary one day was looking for a place to hang her cloak, and she draped it over the rosemary bush. From that day the little flowers took on the same delicate shade of blue.

Some people thought that rosemary, like the Holy Thorn at Glastonbury, bloomed at midnight on Old Christmas Eve. It is said that it grows only for the righteous, and also where the woman is the dominant partner. It has always been a popular evergreen, for the freshness and scent remain long after it is cut. The plant is a symbol of fidelity in love, which makes it particularly suitable for weddings. It stands also for remembrance, and for this reason sprigs were often carried to funerals, to be dropped into the grave, as a promise to remember the dead. The Queen's Maundy Thursday posy contains rosemary and thyme to this day.

Rosemary should never be bought or stolen, but should be presented to the recipient with a little gracious speech, if its good qualities are to be preserved, and bad luck averted.

Old medicinal purposes of rosemary include its use as a plague deterrent. The plant became very expensive during the period of the Black Death, as it was highly sought-after for its healing properties. For gout, poultices of the boiled leaves were said to be a sovereign remedy. It was known as a stimulant, and was good for flatulence, and diseases of the gums and teeth. It was used, too, against epilepsy, memory loss, and dizzy spells. Tisanes and teas were made from the leaves for coughs and many other minor illnesses. Napoleon used large quantities of eau-de-cologne containing oil of rosemary. The oil was known to be harmful if taken in large doses, and was never taken internally more than a few drops at a time. It was, and still is, a favorite ingredient in hair tonics and shampoos. The oil is still used as an insect repellent and in the manufacture of cosmetics.

Rosemary is indigenous to the Mediterranean coast. Its Latin name, *rosmarinus*, means "dew-of-the-sea." It grows best in coastal areas, and enjoys full sun. It is quite happy in rather poor soil as long as there is a little lime in it. It will grow to about three feet high, and can make a pretty, fragrant hedge, or an edging for a large border. There is a dwarf variety, which is prostrate, called *rosmarinus lavandulaceus*. This would be an ideal rockery addition. Rosemary is a traditional cottage garden plant, and a definite must for the herb garden. It is very slow-growing, and best grown from cuttings provided by a gracious friend. Bees love it, and will be attracted to your garden by its presence, helping pollinate everything in sight.

Skin Care

Rosemary is an astringent, and therefore good for excessively oily skin. For a body rub, add some crushed rosemary leaves to a handful of oatmeal. Put this in a little cotton bag, and use it, wetted, to rub over your whole body.

A face rinse for oily skin can be made as follows—boil a handful of rosemary leaves in 1/2 pint water for about five minutes. Let it cool, then strain it. Use it as a freshener on the skin, allowing it to dry on the skin before making-up.

To darken hair and make it shine, add the same mixture to the rinse water.

Present-day uses are culinary as well as cosmetic. Rosemary is traditionally served with lamb, and if you sprinkle a few of the leaves over the lamb joint as it roasts, you will find it adds a delicious flavor. It also goes well with veal. Use it in stuffing, or in a sauce to accompany meat. Chop the leaves finely, or use them whole if preferred, but be careful not to include any of the woody stalks.

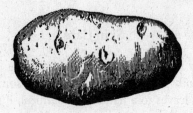

Potatoes with Rosemary

Potatoes, boiled in their jackets till almost
    done
Oil for frying
Sprigs of rosemary
Garlic clove
Salt and pepper

When potatoes are cool, peel and cut into thick slices. Crush the garlic clove. Fry potatoes, garlic, and rosemary leaves all together till browned. Sprinkle with salt and pepper. This is equally delicious if new potatoes are used.

Rosemary Baked Cod

Cod or haddock steaks
Cooking oil
Small onions or shallots
Tomatoes
Chopped rosemary
Salt and pepper

Cut a piece of aluminum foil for each piece of fish (large enough to cover well). Brush foil with oil. Put fish on foil, and sprinkle with salt and pepper. Chop onions and tomatoes and spread on top of fish pieces, with rosemary on top. Put a dash or two of oil over the whole and wrap each piece of foil up like a parcel. Bake on a rack over a tray at 180°C, 350°F or gas mark 4, for about 30 minutes. Delicious!

The Magic of Garlic

By Edain McCoy

As both a magical and medicinal herb, garlic has a long and cherished history. Even modern science, usually the last bastion of medical conservatism, has grudgingly acknowledged the healing powers hidden in garlic.

Garlic remains have been found in burial caves which are at least 10,000 years old. In ancient Greece, garlic was sacred to the crone Goddess, Hecate, and in Rome and France, it was believed to be a potent aphrodisiac. Sailors once wore the herb around their necks to protect from them from both sea monsters and hurricanes. The ancient Egyptians swore sacred oaths with their hands clutching garlic cloves, they used it as currency, and even buried it with their honored dead.

The strongest associations of the herb are with its healing powers, where the boundaries between magic and medicine are considerably blurred. We know that the healing properties of garlic were known at least 5,000 years ago, thanks to a Sumerian cuneiform carving prescribing it for an illness believed to be a common cold.

The Chinese used it as a medicine for treating lung infection, and were the first to take a daily dose as a preventative measure. In

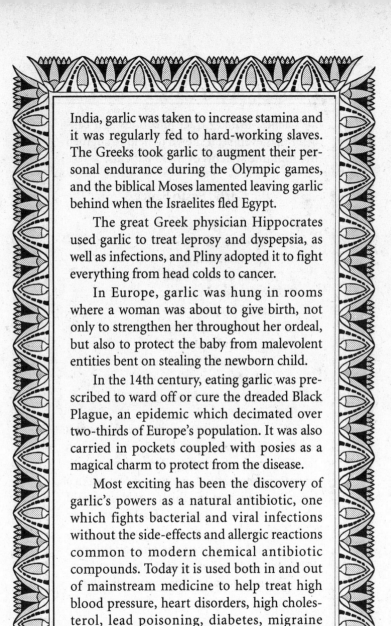

India, garlic was taken to increase stamina and it was regularly fed to hard-working slaves. The Greeks took garlic to augment their personal endurance during the Olympic games, and the biblical Moses lamented leaving garlic behind when the Israelites fled Egypt.

The great Greek physician Hippocrates used garlic to treat leprosy and dyspepsia, as well as infections, and Pliny adopted it to fight everything from head colds to cancer.

In Europe, garlic was hung in rooms where a woman was about to give birth, not only to strengthen her throughout her ordeal, but also to protect the baby from malevolent entities bent on stealing the newborn child.

In the 14th century, eating garlic was prescribed to ward off or cure the dreaded Black Plague, an epidemic which decimated over two-thirds of Europe's population. It was also carried in pockets coupled with posies as a magical charm to protect from the disease.

Most exciting has been the discovery of garlic's powers as a natural antibiotic, one which fights bacterial and viral infections without the side-effects and allergic reactions common to modern chemical antibiotic compounds. Today it is used both in and out of mainstream medicine to help treat high blood pressure, heart disorders, high cholesterol, lead poisoning, diabetes, migraine headaches, urinary tract infections and cancer. It has even been shown to help strengthen the immune systems of AIDS patients.

Garlic Pesto Sauce

1 cup grated Parmesan cheese
1/2 cup olive oil
1/3 cup crushed nuts
2 1/2 cups crushed basil leaves
1/2 cup crushed parsley
3 crushed garlic cloves
1/4 teaspoon crushed
    tarragon leaves
{1/2 cup tomato paste,
    1/4 teaspoon salt, and
    1/4 teaspoon sugar, optional}

Combine all ingredients except the cheese in a medium-sized saucepan. Blend over medium heat while gently stirring. Remove from heat and stir in cheese. Boil one pound of pasta in a large pan of water to which 1 tablespoon of olive oil and 1 teaspoon of salt have been added. (Salt can slow down the boiling process, so add it after the water is already rolling.) When the pasta is done to taste, drain, and cover with the pesto sauce. Serve immediately.

July 7: Tanabata, a Day for Lovers

By Edain McCoy

In Japan there is a legend about two stars perched on opposite sides of the Milky Way. One is called Vega, the little spinning girl who creates the stars, the other is Aquila, the shepherd boy who keeps the stars in their proper formation. Vega and Aquila gaze at each other with longing from across the galaxy. On this one night, the seventh night of the seventh month, they are allowed to come together. Naturally, this makes it a perfect night to take advantage of the romantic energies by casting love spells.

Have Magick, Will Travel: The Marvelous Medicine Bag

By Silver Ravenwolf

Medicine bags have been instruments of magick for centuries. Other appellations for these marvelous bags of magick are spirit bags, mojo bags, conjuring bags, crane bags, and power bags. Their uses include healing, meditation, grounding, psychic work, and prosperity magick.

The medicine bag is a tool that requires close communion with the body. You can wear a small bag on a thong around your neck. Larger medicine pouches can hang from cords or a belt.

Anyone can possess a medicine bag. It does not belong to a particular culture or race of people. It isn't necessary to merit the bag through an oath of dedication or initiation. Representing solitary magick, it is the amplification of the inner you—the self upon the inner journey.

The medicine bag does not have to be of a particular measurement to work. If you relish sizable possessions, then choose or construct a big bag. If you like small, delicate items, then a petite bag would suit your personality. You can purchase medicine bags at numerous spiritual establishments, but do not let anyone lure you with costly jargon on the grounds of authenticity. Only your energy makes the bag authentic. If store-bought turns you off, plan an outing to flea markets and yard sales to unearth the terrific bag for you. The medicine bag, regardless of where or how you find it, should speak to the inner you. Likewise, do not overlook the simple task of making one through your inspirations. An item made by the hands of any magickal individual, whether adept or student, is considered far more powerful than choosing an item off the store shelf.

Paraphernalia to make or decorate the bag can be exotic or simple. Historically, the shaman's bag consisted of hides or pelts sewn with gut or drawn together with a leather thong. Today, animal skins are not necessary for construction of the bag. If you are adverse

Medicine Bag Style #1

Knot the cords together at each side to make drawstrings.

Be sure to leave extra material at the top for a channel to string cords through.

Side A

Side B

Sew side A to side B along outer edges and bottom.

Options: Make side A longer than side B and cut fringes at the bottom. Decorate fringes with beads, shells, feathers or charms.

to the use of animal byproducts, then choose durable cloth instead. The bag can be square or rectangular, sewn on three sides with a draw string top. (See Medicine Bag Style #1.) An option is to cut one side longer than the other and slice the extra material to make fringe. If you desire a different style, you can employ a circular design. Punch holes at intervals near the outside perimeter. Lace with cord running in both directions, then pull to make a pouch. (See Medicine Bag Style #2.) Leather and pelts work particularly well for the circular pouch. To individualize the bag, decorate it with unique stitching, beadwork, buttons, etc.

The contents of the bag are always kept secret. It is not a show-and-tell project. It is a delicate balance of power, serving a specific mystical persona — you! The exception is when a medicine bag is given as a Wiccaning or birthing gift.

Do not worry about filling your medicine bag in one sitting. To begin, select something that represents you now. You could choose a favorite stone, a feather, or a piece of your hair that will link the contents of the pouch to you. Next, find an item that represents the perfect you of your dreams — what you desire to be.

Turn now to the four directions. A brief walk could provide excellent treasures for your bag. The items need not be natural– they do need to signify something to you.

Spiritual connections now come into play. Items that correspond to a favorite deity, energy source, or totem animal also go in the bag. Herbs and incenses for have-magick-will-travel are an excellent addi-

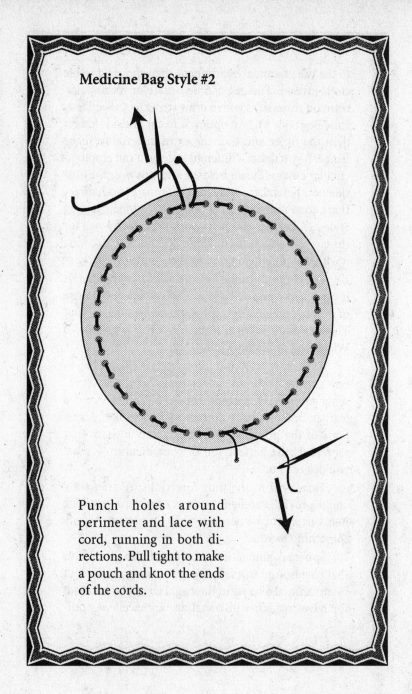

Medicine Bag Style #2

Punch holes around perimeter and lace with cord, running in both directions. Pull tight to make a pouch and knot the ends of the cords.

tion, as well as the ever-potent lodestone, which is useful for both banishing and drawing energies at the magickal person's command. There is no limit to what goes into your medicine bag. Gifts from others are also par excellence for your collection. Over the years, you may bestow from your bag to special individuals. Precious gifts you receive may find their way into your bag.

If you are part of a magickal group, you can spend a delightful evening together making, consecrating, blessing, and filling a bag. It will represent the energies of the group. At later events, display it in a prominent place. Group bags also can be part of a tradition, coven, or group exchange program. If you arrange to go to a festival, or will be participating in a function where several groups will be present, you can make various smaller medicine bags to be given as an exhibit of perfect love and perfect peace among those present.

Your Medicine Bag is the energy of you, here and now. You can draw from it, use it for meditation, cast spells, or ground excess energy into it. It becomes a friend and companion, regardless of your need.

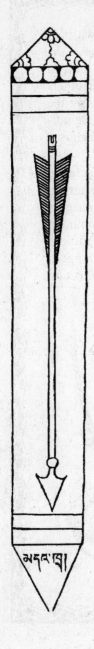

Tibetan Divination

By Patricia Telesco

Tibet is steeped in divination techniques. The "mopa" was the diviner, "lamas," were inspired religious teachers, and "Tulkus" were reincarnated Lamas with strong aptitudes as Seers. Below are some examples of Tibetan divination techniques:

Bird Divination (Bya-rog-kyi-skad-brtag-pa): This technique centers around the crow, believed to be a messenger of the gods. To receive an answer, the querent would voice a question to the winds. The cry of a crow from the southeast meant an enemy is on the way, from the south it meant a visit from a friend, west meant a great wind (change) was soon to come, and from the southwest it was a sign of unexpected profit.

Arrow Divination (Md-mo): Two arrows, one tied with white cloth and the other with black, are used in this oracular attempt. A pile of barley is gathered and placed on a piece of white wool (representing purity). The arrows are thrust into the barley while the petitioner concentrates on the question. As the question is considered, the arrows begin to move. They might fall together, apart, or hit each other, with interpretations for each movement described in holy texts. Movement in the same direction means unified assistance or yes. Movement away is a negative response. If the arrows hit each other, a quarrel or complaint is portended. If they land looking like the hands of a clock, the number indicated is the number of weeks or months until your question is answered.

Butter Lamp Divination (Sman-gsal-mar-me-brtag-pa-ldep): For best results in lamp divination, you should work on the 8th or 10th of the month or during the day of a full or half moon. Take a sliver of wood from a yew-leafed fir tree wrapped in cloth (acts like wick) and place it in the lamp with butter around it. Study the movement of the flame. If the flame is pale, there are problems being caused in your life by karma. If there is black smoke, your vision is obscured and you may not be seeing the truth. If the flame is like a crescent moon, peace and tranquility will be yours. If the smoke smells pleasant, it is a sign of success. Long burning flames are good fortune. Flames shaped like banners mean attainment of a goal. If the flame is dark red and black, there are emotional conflicts in your situation. If the flame is of ugly colors, it means ill health and loss of energy. If it sparks frequently, someone is wishing you evil.

Rosary Divination (Phren-ba): This technique employs the Tibetan version of a rosary (mala) of 108 beads. The mala is held in both hands while the querent tries to open his or her mind to the energies of the moment. The mala is then grasped in two places and beads counted off in equal numbers from each end (usually in groups of

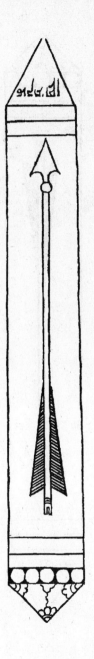

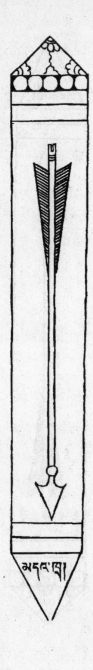

four) until a number between one and four remains. This process is repeated three times, making note of the final number each time.

To perform this yourself, use a yellow cord and make 108 knots in it. Follow the technique given, using these interpretations: One is good fortune, two is misfortune, three is fast movement for boon or bane, and four is moderated goodness with adversity. Each number is augmented by the next one to appear in the reading, so if a querent were to get 1-1-1, it could be considered a very beneficent reading.

The Magic of Wells and Springs

By Mary Brown

St. Augustine struck the ground with his staff and formed a fountain, saying "Cerno Deum" (I see God). So runs the age-old legend about the visit of the great St. Augustine to Cerne Abas in Dorset, England. It is not known if St. Augustine really did visit Dorset when he came from Rome to bring Christianity to these shores, but the "Silver Well" he allegedly fetched out with his staff is still there, ringed by the giant lime trees called the "Twelve Apostles." This was a place of pilgrimage for many centuries, for it had a reputation as a healing well, especially for sore eyes and barren women. It was also a wishing well, where young women could invoke St. Catherine, the patron saint of spinsters, asking her to find them husbands. This holy well of St. Augustine was also said to have oracular powers, so that any who looked into the well on Easter morning would see apparitions of all those who would die in the coming year.

Holy wells and wishing wells are a firmly established feature of our culture. There are at least 800 such wells altogether in the British Isles. Most of

the wells and springs have origins dating back to Pagan times, when water spirits were said to inhabit the wells.

Later, when holy wells were "Christianized," they were often given the name of a Christian saint, but that in itself was not enough to persuade people to abandon all of their old rites and customs. At about the same time, Christian legends began to materialize, such as the one about St. Augustine at Cerne Abas. A great many of the holy wells still in existence, according to legend, had similar beginnings. Other wells sprang up when a saint was martyred nearby, especially if the saint was beheaded. Some wells sprang from the ground where the saint was buried. These holy, if manufactured, connections led to extreme reverence, and wells and springs were popular foci for pilgrimages in the Middle Ages. Like St. Loy's Well at Tottenham, most were said never to fail, even in time of drought. In terms of healing ability, most wells were especially good for eye and skin complaints, and a great many would also relieve barrenness, especially if the dedication was to St. Bride or Bridget, the patron saint of fertility and childbirth.

Wishing wells are found all over the country. One of the most famous is the one at Upwey, near Weymouth in

Dorset, visited in 1789 by George III. The famous mineral springs at Tonbridge, Bath, and Buxton also became popular about this time, and were believed to have healing powers. The Chalice Well at Glastonbury is said to be the place where Joseph of Arimathea buried the Holy Grail.

All over the world there are still wells and springs which have a reputation for healing. In many countries healing wells are found decked with offerings for the water spirit, even if she is ostensibly a Christian saint. Often these offerings take the form of colorful rags, symbolizing the removal of bandages from those who are cured at the well. Such practices are far from dying out, as I found when I visited St. Madron's Well in Cornwall. Traditionally, petitioners at St. Madron's would invoke the Saint's aid by offering pins or pebbles, which were dropped in the well. They would also attempt love divination rituals.

It seems that the magic and mystery of water is still a fascination for us. The rich mixture of Pagan beliefs and Christian legend is an ongoing manifestation of our race-memory. There are still mysteries that we do not fully understand, and which still exert powerful influences, even in a hard-boiled age.

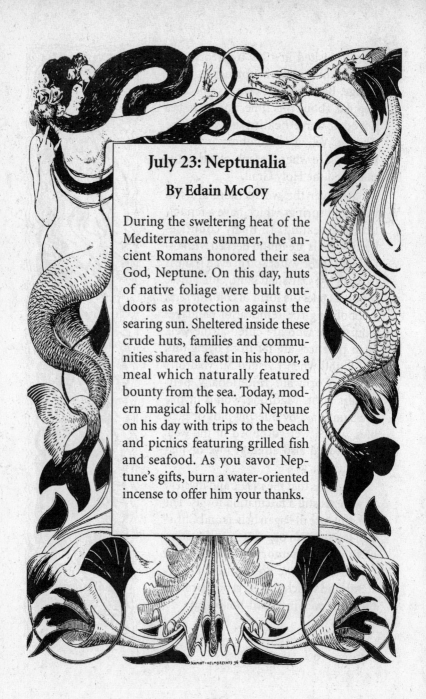

July 23: Neptunalia

By Edain McCoy

During the sweltering heat of the Mediterranean summer, the ancient Romans honored their sea God, Neptune. On this day, huts of native foliage were built outdoors as protection against the searing sun. Sheltered inside these crude huts, families and communities shared a feast in his honor, a meal which naturally featured bounty from the sea. Today, modern magical folk honor Neptune on his day with trips to the beach and picnics featuring grilled fish and seafood. As you savor Neptune's gifts, burn a water-oriented incense to offer him your thanks.

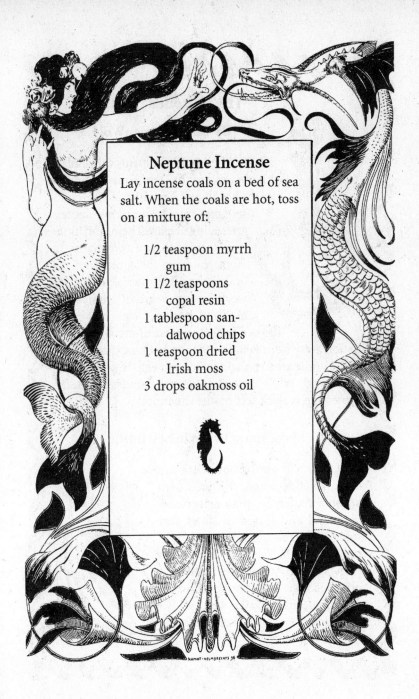

Neptune Incense

Lay incense coals on a bed of sea salt. When the coals are hot, toss on a mixture of:

1/2 teaspoon myrrh
gum
1 1/2 teaspoons
copal resin
1 tablespoon san-
dalwood chips
1 teaspoon dried
Irish moss
3 drops oakmoss oil

The Witches' Bottle

By Silver RavenWolf

The Witches' Bottle is intrinsically linked with the Craft of the Wise. Considered under the heading of sympathetic magick, its uses range from protection to success or healing magick. Their limitations rest only with your creativity. In some cases, as the contents of the bottle chemically break down, or "work," your magickal application jumps into motion. Deteoriating bottles can banish sickness or move a bad situation away from you. In other operations, the contents of the bottle are to remain intact, protected from the outside world. While the contents remain undisturbed, the protection magick secures the situation.

Make Your Own Witches' Bottle

First, you will need a bottle. It can be large, small, colored, designed — it doesn't matter. Keep an assortment from tall and fluted to short and squat. Sealed bottles require a tight cap. Bottles that need air circulation should have a lid with punched holes to allow the aroma to escape. Small jelly jars with canning lids are a good choice to begin. Now you must focus on the type of magickal operation you will employ. Is this to heal a friend, pay off the electric bill, or protect your best friend while she vacations? Choosing the contents to match your desire is the next step. The list below will give you an idea of the types of items to put in the bottle. All bottles should be cleansed, consecrated, filled, and empowered within a magick circle.

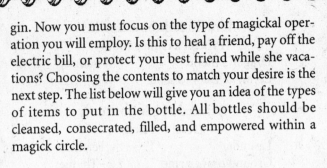

Sealed Witches' Bottle
(Banish unwanted situations)

Needles & Pins	Rosemary
Angelica	Vinegar
Garlic	

Sealed Siren's Bottle
(Banish unwanted influences)

Broken shells	Seaweed
Driftwood	Sea Water
Sand	

Aerated Boogie Bottle
(Scare away unwanted ghosties)

Nails	Angelica
Red Yarn and	Garlic
Black Yarn tied in knots	

Open Stone Sucker Bottle
(Collect negativity)

Pebbles	Stones
Dirt	Rosemary

Aerated Rainbow Bottle
(Protect a child's room)

Dragon's Blood   Rosemary
Layers of colored sand

Aerated Spirit Bottle
(Heal the sick)

Lavender   Feathers
Ground orange rind   Thyme
Ground orange peels

Aerated Bottle of Wealth
(Bring Money)

Silver   Cinquefoil
Cinnamon Oil

Aerated PMS Bottle
(Pre-menstrual tension)

Jasmine   Sage
Cinnamon   Rose
Orange peel   Moonstone

August 1: The Festival of Green Corn

By Edain McCoy

While European-oriented Pagans are celebrating August 1 as Lammas, a festival of the first harvest, Native North Americans are observing a similar holiday of their own. Like Lammas, the Festival of Green Corn is a communal event, largely honoring the newly-cut grains. The Native peoples enact ancient, sacred rituals to thank the Corn Grandmother for her bounty, and make mock sacrifices of the grain in her honor. Rough competitive games are played while the feast is being prepared, then the tribe dines together on rich foods and breads made from the newly-harvested corn. After everyone is full, the community gathers for traditional storytelling.

Harvest Home

By Mary Brown

Dry August and warm
Doth harvest no harm.

This is the roasted, dried-out husk of summer—flowers are drying and withering, their seed-pods rattling. The undergrowth is browned and worn out by the fierce rays of the summer sun. The wheat fields stand bulging ripe and golden, ready for the scythe, or rather, these days, ready for the combine harvester. As a child I helped in the fields at harvest time, as did many other country children, following behind the rather primitive mowing machine and tying the loose straw into sheaves. These sheaves were then propped up into golden "stooks" and left to dry thoroughly in the baking sun. Later the sheaves would be stacked onto high wagons and taken off to the farmyard to await threshing, or sometimes they were made into a rick in the corner of the field. Several shouting, sweating men would stand atop the ever-growing rick, while we poor laborers at the bottom had to pitch the sheaves as fast as we could onto the clattering elevator. The men on top arranged the rick in the special way required to protect it from the weather. At lunch-time it was bread and cheese all round and swigs of cold tea from a bottle, for we children were not allowed the rough cider the men drank.

The weather was crucial, for a certain number of dry days was needed to get the harvest in safely. Anxious farmers continually scanned the skies at this time, to judge whether they should start to cut, or whether it would be best to leave it a few days. Either way meant risk, for heavy rains could damage the crop irreparably. Today things are different; huge combine harvesters can cut and process the corn in the space of a few days, and there are many artificial aids to ensure that the crop is kept in perfect condition. The fields look different too, for no longer do the red poppies wave in abundance—pesticides have seen to that. No longer do ricks stand in the corners of the fields—instead great black polythene rolls of hay are all that remain to show for the field crops.

Three hundred years ago the time of harvest was a most joyful occasion, celebrated by a great harvest supper like the one described so vividly in Hardy's *Far From the Madding Crowd*. For the farm laborers,

harvest-time was the most concentrated period of work in the farming year, with all members of the family fully employed around the clock till the work was done. As the last high-piled wagon or "hock-cart" lumbered into the rick-yard, the cry would go up, "Harvest home–Harvest home." The mood was joyful; the young men and girls decked out in straw crowns, full of happy anticipation for the Harvest Supper whichwould soon follow. A good time was had by all, with the groaning board holding more food than most laboring people would see in a year.

Going back even further, to the time of our Celtic ancestors, August was "Lugnasad," one of the four great festivals of the year. The word comes from "Lugh," the Sun god, and "nasad," an assembly. Like all the ancient festivals, this celebration was later "Christianized," becoming Lammas or "loaf mass." Traditionally, small loaves were made from the first fruits of the harvest for eating at a ceremonial meal. In Scotland, the loaves were cooked over a rowan fire. They were then distributed and eaten, after which the celebrants paraded sunwise round the fire. Lammastide was an important Quarter Day in the Middle Ages, but this is now only remembered in Scotland, for Celtic remnants survived much longer in the Celtic fringes than in the rest of the British Isles. Lammastide fairs were often held on ancient hilltop forts or earthworks, showing that their origins stretch far back into the ages. All were great cattle and sheep fairs, and great occasions for country folk to enjoy rough games and amusement stalls and to buy fripperies.

By the end of August, the harvest is complete. The fertility figure, the Corn Dolly, has been made from the last sheaf of corn, and hung up in the house to ensure a good harvest for next year. As the first cut of the plough is made on Plough Monday, she will be ploughed in to bring continuity and fertility to the soil once again. The Corn Spirit, who hid in the last sheaf of corn, the White Goddess, Mother Earth, and St. Bride all have connections with the Corn Dolly, or "Kern Baby" as she is sometimes called. In Scotland they call her "the maiden," but however she is known, she epitomizes the curious mix of superstition, tradition, and almost forgotten religious ceremony which attends our ancient agricultural way of life and its seasonal turning points.

After this climax, all that remains is the apple harvest, and the gathering of every kind of fruit and nut, to build up the winter stores. The glorious summer is at an end and the Earth will sleep until re-awakened by the smile of the returning Sun-god in the spring.

August 22: Tij, a Holiday for Women

By Edain McCoy

Looking for a magical alternative to the blatant commercialism of our modern Mother's Day? Then why not adopt Tij, a Nepalese festival which honors all women? On the full moon of August, no woman in Nepal is permitted to labor. The youngest girls and male members of the family pitch in to do whatever household work needs to be done, and women who outside the home are usually given the day off. With roots in ancient Pagan beliefs, the women honor themselves as living representations of the Goddess.

Magical Apple Lore

By Edain McCoy

The simple red apple holds an esteemed place in European myth and legend, and is linked to many well-known Goddesses. Most prominent is the Roman deity Pamona, the Goddess of apples and of the fruit harvest. In Irish myth, an apple tree grows over the grave of the maiden Goddess Aillin. This tree grew up to entwine with the yew tree of her lover, Baile.

In folklore, how an apple is presented often tells us much about the hidden Goddess. Whole apples, juicy and life-giving on the outside but concealing the deadly cyanide-filled seeds, are the province of the crone, as is seen in the tale of Snow White. When cut crosswise to show the five pointed star inside, the apple represents mother Goddesses—such as in the

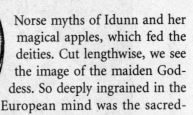

Norse myths of Idunn and her magical apples, which fed the deities. Cut lengthwise, we see the image of the maiden Goddess. So deeply ingrained in the European mind was the sacredness of the apple that the early church fathers were forced to deliberately change the infamous fruit of the Biblical Garden of Eden from a generic fruit (probably an apricot or fig in that part of the world) into an apple, in order to demonize its appeal.

In old Scandinavia and in the Celtic countries, apples were signs of life and rebirth. They were frequently buried as symbolic living sacrifices to the deities in order to ensure the continuance of earthly life. In Ireland, it was traditional in the weeks before Samhain (October 31) to slice an apple in two, mentally pour an illness, problem, or bad habit into its meaty center, then put it back together and bury it in the ground to rid oneself of the unwanted attribute.

The Halloween game of bobbing for apples was taken from an old Pagan need to capture the essence of the old Goddess, who is allowing the world to die into winter as she grieves for her dead consort. To grasp the slippery fruit was an act of sympathetic magic, enacted to ensure her returned interest when she gave birth anew to her beloved God.

In old Wales, apples represented the human soul. The most common name for the land of the dead in the Welsh language is Avalon, meaning "land of apples." At Samhain the red fruit was ritually buried to feed the dead souls of family and friends while they waited in the Underworld for rebirth.

In Ireland, on the first Sunday in September, many rural Irish still observe an old Pagan festival called Garland Sunday. Villagers tie shiny red apples to a long length of green garland and parade to the local cemetery. Once there, the apples are dispersed upon the graves as magical wishes for life renewed.

With all the Pagan lore linked to the simple, it is little wonder that the fruit has been used for centuries as a catalyst for magic and divination. If you are single and curious about your romantic future, on Samhain night, try walking backwards into a dimly lit room while eating an apple. Turn and glance into a mirror where the face of your true love should appear.

If poverty is your bane, tie a string to a coin and press it deep within the center of a fresh apple. Hang the fruit up and, without using your hands, try to bite out the coin. An Irish legend says that if you can manage this feat your pockets will be overflowing with money in the coming year.

The easiest way to release apple magic is to dry apples and hang the slices on cords made of fishing line, or by gluing or wiring them to wreath forms found in craft supply stores. If you have no immediate magical need, the dried apples still make lovely seasonal decorations with which to honor the Goddess of the Harvest.

To dry apples, cut them into 1/4 inch thick slices. These can be whole or half cuts depending on which catches your fancy. Soak them for an hour in a brine made of 1 cup lemon juice, 2 tablespoons salt, 1 tablespoon vinegar, and 2 cups water. Spread these on an ungreased cookie sheet and bake in your oven for three hours at 175 to 200 degrees. After three hours, turn off the oven, but do not remove the apples. Allow them to sit for another two or three days either in this, or in some other warm place. After this time they will be fully dried and will last almost forever!

Tea To'tlers' Wine

By Patricia Telesco

It's fun to prepare a special tea wine. Here is one recipe:
- 1 gallon water
- 15 tea bags (your choice of flavor)
- 3 to 4 pounds of sugar or honey
- 1 lemon, sliced
- 1 orange, sliced
- 1/2 inch ginger root, bruised
- 1/2 package active yeast (wine yeast is best)

Boil the water, then add the tea to steep. Steep for 20 minutes. Remove tea bags and add sugar or honey. Heat over low flame until sugar or honey is dissolved.

Turn the heat off and add the lemon, orange, and ginger. Cover and cool to lukewarm. Meanwhile, dissolve yeast in 1/4 cup of warm water. Add this to the tea, covering the pot with a terry cloth towel for 24 hours. Remove the ginger, lemon, and orange , and allow the beverage to sit at room temperature for another two days.

Pour into sterilized bottles and cork loosely. Leave this for two weeks, then strain again and place in sterilized airtight containers to age for 8 months to one year. The earlier aging yields a sweeter wine.

Hint: Do not add less sugar or honey to your mixture because it tastes too sweet. Yeast needs the sugar to produce alcohol. The longer the wine ferments, the drier the finished wine becomes.

What Do You Mean, Your Spells Don't Work?

By Silver RavenWolf

Spell casting, in and of itself, is not difficult. Generally, it follows an easy formula with separate and distinct steps. A spell is a procedure to follow to reach a desired end. It does not require a great deal of money, a huge compendium of tools, or exotic ingredients to work. It does require faith in yourself and a connection with deity.

When describing spells to non-magickal people, a witch will often tell them that a spell is much like a prayer. You are calling upon divinity to assist you, as in a prayer, but a spell requires more than just pleading to divinity to help you out of a jam. In a spell *you* are an active ingredient. Your faith and your knowledge are as important as understanding there is divinity out there to call upon.

Many of you have already heard of the Witches' Pyramid, the foundation of our magickal acts: To Know, To Will, To Dare, and To Be Silent. This pyramid is the underlying structure of any spell formula.

To Know

Before you can cast a spell, you need to know who you are. Ego aside, you have to come to terms with who you are, how you operate, and why you do the things you do.

The second thing you must know is precisely what you want. This is not as easy as it seems. People rarely sit back and consider what they really want out of life. Part of this is because they are afraid. They fear they may not get what they want, and they fear that they will fail. These fears stop us from knowing.

For example, time and again people I know have spelled for love. They have not done the ultimate no-no by targeting a specific person, but they do something just as bad — they don't really know what they ultimately want. When they get what they spelled for, often they are disappointed, because there is something attached to that new lover they didn't think of. Therefore, all spells must be specific.

One of the best ways to begin a working is to write out, in detail, exactly what you want in one straight line on a piece of paper. Underneath, phonetically begin to pare each word down. Underneath that line, pare the words down again. Continue this procedure until only one letter from each word is left. Interlock the few remaining letters into a sigil. Use this sigil in whatever magickal application you have chosen to ensure your spell remains specific.

To Will

Another stumbling block in spell casting is lack of will, whether it is will power, belief, or conviction. Will depends on how badly you want to make a change. Do you believe you are capable of making the change, or do you think it is only wishful thinking? Are you willing to reprogram your mind, your environment, your relationships, in order to bring about the change you desire? Without will, a spell will fizzle. Is your mind clogged with doubt, or unnecessary problems that will prevent bringing about the change you say you want?

One of the best techniques for increasing your will power is the use of meditation on a daily basis. Once you have learned to relax, use the alpha state to program the events you wish to come to pass. You should work on both short-term and long-term goals.

Another technique that is useful in spell casting is to write down why you wish to manifest something. Let this explanation sit on your altar overnight, then re-read it. Does it make sense? Is this what you really want? Does your reasoning still appear firm, or is it full of holes?

Are you patient? Patience has a lot to do with will. Once you have a firm grip on "will," you are a third of the way through on accurate spell casting.

To Dare

To dare means you are not inclined to sit around on your laurels. It means that you are not choosing to procrastinate, rather you are choosing to move with purpose. To dare indicates that you are no longer afraid of the outcome, or fear failure. You are confident that you control your own destiny to the point where you won't even argue about it, either with someone else, or yourself.

Although "to dare" doesn't appear to create lot of work, it does require you to make an active decision. This is the next catalyst for your magickal operation. From here, you will plan the appropriate day, hour, moon phase, astrological energies, and tools required for working magick, including what divinity you will choose. To dare can lead to a great deal of work and preparation.

To Be Silent

Even if you are an adept, you should learn to be quiet about your magickal operations. There is only one exception, which is when you are working with a group. If the group mind is actively participating on a project they should be informed of their success or failure.

In the beginning, you should be silent so that you are not affected by others' opinions. Don't tell them what you are performing magick for, as you risk failure. Why? Because they can unconsciously affect you with their disbelief or negativity.

Likewise, once you become proficient at spell casting, don't announce it — especially to a novice. No real adept will ever tell a novice that "My spells always work." Not only is it rude, it is also untrue. Everyone fails. Imagine what a novice would think if they knew you lost your job, your kids are running rampant, and you are deeply in debt. If your spells always worked, you would not be in such a fix, would you? Foolish words can ruin your reputation, which in turn, will ruin your own self-confidence. Therefore, keep your trap shut — this ensures success on your magickal operations as well as keeping your reputation intact. No one likes a braggart, and no one considers an egotistical Witch a good leader or cleric.

Drawing by Susan Baxter

Hair Superstitions

By D.J. Conway

✂ Men with very hairy arms and hair on the backs of their hands were believed to be able to become wealthy.

✂ If a man's hair grows down on his forehead and back above the temples, it was said he would live to a very old age.

✂ Curly hair is said to be the mark of a lucky person.

✂ Women who cut their hair only during the Waxing Moon were said to draw good luck. If cut during the Waning Moon, it would lose its luster and fall out.

✂ The widow's peak meant the woman would outlive her first husband and remarry soon.

✂ If a woman with straight hair suddenly had two curls on her forehead, her husband was cheating on her.

✂ In India, a man without hair on his chest was thought to be, or would become, a thief.

✂ If you suddenly lose a lot of hair, it is a sign of financial problems and bad health.

✂ A loose hair on your shoulder means a letter is coming.

✂ In the United States, it was once a popular belief that thinning hair was caused by a hat that was too tight. It was also said that shaving the head closely was a cure for baldness.

✂ Beware of that man, Be he friend or brother, Whose hair is one color, And mustache is another. The same is said about beards which are not the same color as the hair.

✂ Under Elizabeth I of Britain, being clean-shaven became popular because the queen levied a tax on beards.

✂ Rum poured onto the hair will make it curly.

✂ An old Russian proverb says: There was never a saint with red hair.

Wells: A Deep Subject

By Patricia Telesco

Water taken from three different wells, if poured half on the ground and then administered to the sick, will cure fever.

The water of the well of Culloden Heath in Scotland is believed to bring good fortune if you drink it on New Year's Day. Always leave a coin in thankfulness for your blessing.

If you skim the water from a neighbor's well as the dawn breaks on May Day, you can snatch his or her prosperity for the coming year.

St. Oswald's well is believed to be able to divine a patient's health. Here, a piece of clothing is tossed upon the waters. If it floats, the patient will recover fully. A swatch of this garment is then left in a nearby tree to thank the Saint for the insight.

If you gently float a small dish in a well and concentrate on a question, a clockwise spin is a positive answer. Counterclockwise is negative, and no movement is uncertainty.

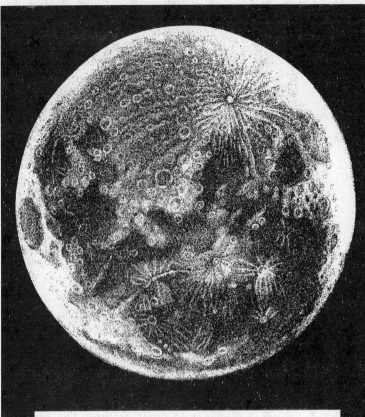

September 19: The Festival
of Chang-O
By Edain McCoy

On the Full Moon nearest the autumnal equinox, the Chinese pay homage to the moon Goddess Chang-O. The holiday—which is celebrated with feasting, music, divinations, and the retelling of her myth—features her sacred number of thirteen. Thirteen is the number of Full Moons in the solar year, each lunation representing her benevolent appearance over the Earth.

Attuning Your Home With Dragon Energy

By D.J. Conway

Has your home, property, or business been plagued with a long series of disruptions and misfortunes? Have you, your family, and your pets been subjected to one illness after another? You say that all your magickal endeavors haven't helped, and your protection rituals never seem to quite take full effect. Have you considered that the dragon energy of your immediate area may be disrupted in some way?

Unlike the later European cultures, the ancient Chinese thought of dragons as wise and helpful creatures. This very old civilization firmly believed in controlling what they call "dragon's breath" in the landscape and architecture. This is still a respected belief in Hong Kong and other places having Chinese communities. The professionals who are adept at finding imbalance of the dragon's breath are called Feng-shui diviners. They are in demand by both home and business owners.

Suppose a series of unexplained illnesses or misfortunes strikes a business or home. The owner will go through the ordinary procedures to discover a cause. If nothing logical is found, he will send for a person skilled in detecting a disruption of this dragon's breath energy.

The Feng-shui diviner will go to the home or business and take sighting along what are called the veins of the dragon. These veins are often raised features of the landscape, such as trees, rocks, watercourses, valleys, hills, etc. Inside the buildings, the diviner will consider such things as doorways, halls, the directions of corners, placement of furniture, and whether the building is situated at true angles to the compass directions.

Whatever the diviner recommends to the owner is seriously implemented. Often, a small garden is made outside for the dragon of that particular site. Inside, a small shrine may be placed in a particular area or corner for the dragon. Images of dragons are placed in both the garden and the shrine as a token of respect by the human residents.

However strange all this may seem to Westerners, the Chinese who have implemented such advice will tell you that the problems stopped and the prosperity of home and business improved.

The Chinese say that these lines, or flows of dragon's breath (chi) exist in all parts of the world. The British call these ley lines. Modern European dowsers call the disrupted lines of energy "black radiations," saying that these affect the landscape, vegetation, and crops, and any humans and animals that live in that area. They "stake" the black radiations with metal rods to restore the proper balance and flow of energy, much as an acupuncturist does on the human body.

These lines of dragon's breath can be straight for several miles, then meander from one direction to another. This is not an automatic signal that the line is disrupted. This seems to be a natural phenomena of such lines of dragon energy.

Even if you were fortunate enough to find a Feng-shui diviner, I'm not certain you could persuade him/her to help a Westerner. The best recourse is to correct the imbalance yourself.

Get a compass and a large pad of paper for your observations. First, determine if your home or business is set to the true compass directions. Most buildings are not set true, but angled at strange positions to fit the lot, city planning, or the street. There isn't much you can do about changing this, but will have to compensate by making certain adjustments inside.

Next, check to see if your front and back doors are exactly opposite each other, with a hallway or clear space connecting them. If they are, you need to interrupt this clear passage. The Chinese say that such a straight-through arrangement disrupts the flow of dragon energy and allows all your good luck and balance to run out of the building. This is the reason that many Oriental residences have a decorative screen set a few feet inside, blocking the door from the rest of the house. You can do some major remodeling, or you can use some other less expensive techniques.

If the front door opens directly into a room, consider the Chinese device of a large folding screen to separate the door from the room. You might hang a large mirror facing the door, so that the reflection will allow the dragon energy time to readjust itself before running on through. If possible, place a small table under the mirror. On this table arrange a plant, fresh or dried flowers, or an artistic arrangement of stones in a bowl along with a statue of a dragon.

If you found that your house was not set true to the compass directions, you will need to consider placing furniture in the corners of the rooms. Any object set in a corner will keep the dragon energy from pooling there and turning sour, or negative. A chair or sofa set across a corner, instead of into it, will work just fine.

If you find that you don't like the furniture in such positions, find some powerful crystals or stones and place them in the corners. Just be certain that the stones have a strong positive charge to them. Positive-powered crystals and stones will redirect the energy and balance it.

Not all corners are likely to collect sour energy. By using a pendulum you can determine which corners are the most negative. Be sure you understand before trying this what the pendulum swings mean. You might designate forward and backward for positive, sideway for negative, or sunwise circling for positive and widdershins for negative.

Outside, check for little hollows in the yard, the placement of certain trees, or any areas where water runs, even if it is only seasonal. Plant flowers or herbs in or around these places if the pendulum indicates a collection of negative energy. Decorate these places with shells and stones.

You can also help the dragon's breath energy flow by planting little flower or herb gardens in other areas of your yard that you find to be negatively charged. In a manner of speaking, this garden and arrangement will be an outdoor shrine to the dragon of your immediate area.

By taking a little time and effort, you can correct the flow of dragon energy through your home and property. Once corrected from negative to positive, these energy flows will attract friendly spirits, the Little People, and of course, dragons!

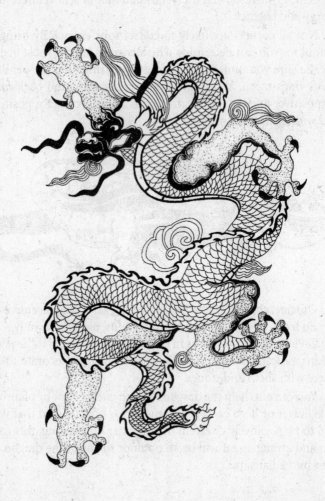

14. LA TEMPERANCE

Fun Things with the Tarot

By Silver RavenWolf

I understand you love working with your tarot deck, but you want to know if there is something more you can do with it? Of course there is!

Tell a Story. Choose a card you are having difficulty with and make up a story. It can be any kind you pick. When you are finished, put the story and the card under your pillow before you go to sleep *or* put it on your altar. Not only will you understand the card better in the future, you may even hit upon a great tale to be told to friends later!

Pick A Card, Any Card. This is great for family reunions, birthday parties, or New Year's Eve Bashes. Fan the tarot deck and ask the first person to pick a card. This card will stand for the energies he or she will most need to stay in touch with during the year.

Use your tarot cards as props in spellcasting and ritual work. For example, if you are looking for abundance in your life, choose the Ace of Pentacles, the Ten of Pentacles, and the Empress. Put them in the center of your altar, or on a table where they will not be disturbed. In a magic circle, burn a gold candle and meditate on bringing abundance toward yourself and your family.

Spend an evening developing your own tarot spreads. Not everyone accesses the astral in the same way, nor do they draw conclusions in the same manner. Design spreads that are specifically for your use. Perhaps there will be one you will use quite often. It may become your trademark!

Are your readings sometimes muddled? Have a divinatory tool nearby that is not the tarot. I suggest something like the Cartouche or Rune cards so that the querent (the person you are reading for) can see the cards, too. If an area is cloudy, put down the other type of card on top of the tarot card to give you more insight.

Ever get one of those people who likes to play "Test the Card Reader?" You can stop this by asking their birth day *before* they come to see you. Utilize astrology or numerology to prepare for any querent. You don't have to be a crack astrologer to glean good information.

Hone your skills by working with numerous decks. Every deck has something new to share, a different way of perceiving an issue. Keep careful notes for yourself.

Use a double deck when reading. I read with a double deck for an entire summer. The results were most interesting. Double cards showed areas that needed to be stressed for the querent. To make things really interesting, mix two decks (they will have to be the same brand). Without looking, choose 72 cards. Do a few readings with them. Watch the interesting things that pop up.

Design your own deck of tarot cards. Blank decks can be purchased at New Age or Metaphysical book stores. Begin collecting pictures of what the various cards mean to you. You will be delighted with the outcome and it is a treasure to keep. In fact, you may find it such an enjoyable pastimet that you design decks for friends using pictures they give you, plus things you find.

Make a game out of your cards. Design a board game or write a computer program. This is a great way to teach your children the meanings of the cards. It can be as simple or as difficult as you wish.

October 31: Lating Night

By Edain McCoy

The Old Religion was demonized in Medieval England in order to lessen its appeal to the masses, and no vestige of the Old Ways was more trounced upon than Samhain/Halloween. This festival, which honored and celebrated the dead and gave us hope for life renewed, was made into a night of rampant evil, presided over by the king of all evil, the Christian Satan. Until well into this century, rural English folk would hide indoors on Samhain, cowering in fear of the malevolence which they were sure lay just beyond their thresholds.

In East Anglia, a curious communal custom for detecting the cloaked evil that stalked the land was born, and Samhain eve was redubbed "Lating Night." The term is thought to derive from the word "latent," meaning that which lurks or is hidden.

Just before midnight, the brave rural folk would carry white candles out over their fields, into the woods, and across the peaks of the faery hillocks. If their candles burned steady and true, there was no evil present. but if the flames sputtered, sparked, or died, it was a sure sign that something wicked was afoot, and the local religious officials would be called upon to exorcise the evil from the particular area.

Today's magical folk can reclaim this custom for our own. If you feel any sort of negative energy has become attached to your land, take your white candle and make the slow trek across it, all the while gauging the reactions of the flame. If you come upon a place where you suspect negativity has settled, sprinkle a purifying solution of water, salt, and lemon juice over the area in question while saying:

Night winds howl and goblins crow,
All evil here will have to go.
Sputter like flame, your dying light,
Depart, oh wicked sprites, this night.

Who's Afraid of the Big Bad Crone?

By Silver RavenWolf

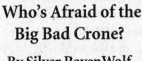

Throughout history, dark goddesses dance among the shadows of human memory. There is Lilith—She of the Chasms of Sexuality, and Sekhmet, full-bodied Egyptian with a roar that shatters the evil in humans, destroying them completely and sending them to another realm. There is Coatlicue, the Aztec Mother/Crone Goddess clothed in feathers and human hearts. There is Kali, the bloodthirsty bride of Shiva and savior of women in peril. Hecate guards our crossroads and brings us justice, while the Morrigan dances into our battles and seduces great warriors. These, and many more, are the ever present, big, bad crones.

Kali

I've been studying them for quite some time. In fact, I began working with them because someone said, "Ouuu, you like her? Well, I've got news for you. You don't pick the Morrigan. She picks you. Personally, I think she's ugly."

Awesome. The choice was mutual.

Dark goddess work and Crone energy require only two considerations from the magickal practitioner—respect and a strong sense of ethics. If you stray from your values and principles, you will be in for an interesting, if not frightful ride, but if you work with honesty and integrity, then the boundaries of magickal applications with the dark goddesses are limitless.

What kind of work can you do with these ladies of the deep?

You can access your darker side through meditation and learn to understand what makes you tick, what to improve in yourself, what to eliminate, what to direct more energy to. You can aspect them to catch pushers, rapists, murderers and thieves.

I kid you not.

Dark Goddess energy is excellent for protection magick. You think I jest? Well, let me tell you two stories about Kali. One of the first things I teach anyone who comes to me is how to call Kali when they are in trouble. By trouble, I mean when you find yourself in a situation of violence that you did not create, but has come knocking at your Karma anyway. Simply stand straight, legs apart and call "Kali" in a very loud voice, I tell them. Of course, they think I'm nuts, until they find themselves in a predicament.

Rita's story: "Thank Goddess you told me about Kali. I had to work late one evening. On my way home I realized that I'd forgotten to fill up the gas tank and found myself forced to stop at a self-serve I don't normally frequent. I pumped the gas and headed into the little store. There were two guys loitering outside. They did some name calling as I went in, but didn't follow me. I paid for the gas, but was nervous about going back out there, so I hung around in the store

Sekhmet

235

Coatlicue

for awhile. When I thought the parking lot empty, I headed out.

"They were still there. I was afraid I would not make it across the parking lot to my car. To be honest, fear gnawed at my guts. Then I remembered what you told me. I turned around and yelled 'Kali' at the top of my lungs. As I did so, the fellow sitting in his cab dropped his hot coffee all over his lap, and the one standing by the building got smacked in the face by a snowball. You know, there was no one, I mean not a soul, around who could have thrown that snowball. I didn't worry about it though. I just thanked the Goddess under my breath, ran across the parking lot and scrambled in my car. I took off like the hounds of the hunt were after me. They never moved to follow."

Carrie's story: "I was out on a photo shoot in the middle of nowhere with a photographer — a big guy I'd worked with before. He was supposed to be one of the agency's best. None of the other women had ever said anything bad about him other than that he was a bag of wind. The shoot wasn't going well and we were ready to pack up. I'll never forget the scene as long as I live. One minute everything was calm, the next minute the photographer had me in a bear grip. He told me how he had wanted to do this for a long time.

"My heart was pounding and my brain shocked into disbelief. I now understand why rabbits freeze in the headlights of on-coming cars destined to squish them on the highway. I don't know how long I remained standing there like an idiot. Finally, I struggled. It only made the entire situation worse.

My mind desperately grasped on what I should be doing rather than what I was doing. In my head, I screamed for Kali.

"The strangest thing happened. He stopped, picked up his camera bag, and sheepishly ran his hand over his face. 'I'm so sorry,' he stammered. 'I don't know what got into me.'

"To this day, I don't know how I got out of that situation unscathed, but I thank Kali every chance I get."

Dark goddeses with wise energy, wrapping us in a cloak of self-empowerment.

Are you afraid of the big, bad crone?

Not.

Incenses to Assist in Conjuring Spirits

By Edain McCoy

Ancient grimoires contain tantalizing references to incenses which the old Magi and Witches used to facilitate contact with the spirit world. Some believed that the incense itself created a portal through which the spirit could travel to the earth plane, others that the vibrations of the herbs merely opened the psychic "eye" to the unseen world, which is always present, but normally invisible.

Many of the herbs thought to be most efficacious in spirit contact were deadly and, sadly, the darker side of history is punctuated with the quick and premature deaths of those who breathed in the poisonous fumes.

The following recipes are for traditional incenses which are made with non-toxic substances. The measurements are for pre-ground, dried herbs, with proportions designed to fit on a charcoal incense block about one to two inches across. The scent will carry for 15 to 20 minutes. Increase ingredients as needed for covering larger surfaces, or if you wish the incense to burn longer.

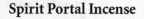

Spirit Portal Incense

1/2 teaspoon cinnamon
1/2 teaspoon lavender
a pinch of wormwood

Attunement to Spirit World Incense

1/4 teaspoon ground sandalwood, or
1/2 teaspoon of sandalwood chips
1/4 teaspoon Balm of Gilead
1/8 teaspoon sage

Opening Eyes to Spirit World Incense

1/3 teaspoon mastic
1/3 teaspoon amaranth
1/3 teaspoon yarrow

Keep in mind that you need to protect yourself and your working area, particularly when our intent is to open a portal between worlds. You don't want just anyone—or anything—coming through. Always work with spirits from within the confines of your magic circle, while keeping your thoughts focused on attracting only those discarnates whose intent toward you is loving and helpful. Tossing in a pinch of frankincense with any of the above recipes is another excellent way to keep low entities at bay and further protect yourself and your working space.

Unleashing the Magic in Your Fireplace

By Edain McCoy

Throughout old Europe, the fireplace was the center of the home, both literally and emotionally. Over its blazing embers meals and medicines were prepared, by its warm glow families gathered to eat and converse, and it provided the primary source of heat and light on cold, dark nights. Little wonder that the humble fireplace has been liberally used as a focus for myth-making and magic. Try some of these simple, but effective, magical ideas in your own hearth:

Folktales always portray the fireplace flue as the magical entry to one's home. When there is no fire, use the cold chimney as a portal for channeling spirits into your presence.

Add wormwood or yew (yew is toxic!) to the fire to summon the dead.

Hanging a wreath over the fireplace opening will protect the chimney from acting as an open portal for uninvited spirits. Crossing your fireplace tools in front of the open hearth, or placing your magical broom lengthwise in front of it, will also block the portal.

Burn an oak log to aid someone under your roof in overcoming a debilitating illness.

Burn a pine log to bring prosperity to those under your roof.

Tossing spicy, fragrant herbs—such as cloves or orange peels—on the flames will impart magical protection to your home.

Laying the fire on a foundation of sea salt is also protective.

Collect the fire's ashes for making protection talismans, or scattering around the outside of the home to protect the grounds.

Burn elder wood to protect from baneful spirits, or to attract friendly faery folk to your hearthside.

Setting an offering of milk near a warm firplace will also draw beneficial faery life to your home.

Spring flowers added to the fire make a perfect catalyst for spells to bring romance into your life.

Dogwood blossoms tossed in the hot embers of a dying fire, along with the name of an enemy, will cause him to lose interest in you.

Write the name of someone you wish to banish from your life in dragon's blood on a piece of dark paper and toss it in the fire. Within a lunar month, the person should move away.

Burning three red ribbons one-by-one will banish the attentions of an unwanted suitor. Burning three green or pink ones will bring him or her back.

Sprinkling eyebright onto the blaze will make the flame conducive to psychic work, especially scrying.

Toss sandalwood chips into the fire to psychically purify the area.

Don't Have a Fireplace? Build a Hearth!

By Silver RavenWolf

Not all of us are fortunate enough to have our own fireplaces. Here are some ideas, ranging from expensive to dirt cheap, to give you that "home and hearth" feel.

1. Purchase a small wood stove.

2. Purchase an electric fireplace and surround it with flagstone.

3. Choose a corner of your room and fit pieces of flagstone together. Place an oil lamp on the flagstone. (Take safety precautions—this is not a good idea forhomes with kids or pets). You can even plug in a hot plate to simmer brews and potions.

4. For outside—build a small circle of stone and put your grill in the center.

Fires and Feasting

By Mary Brown

he ancient Celts celebrated the end of the farming year at Samhain. It was a time for killing surplus animals, taking stock, and mating the sheep for next year's lambing. Harvests were in, and preparations made for the long, hard winter. It was time to light great bonfires and sacrifice lambs, for the gods came close to the Earth at this turning point of the year.

The ancient fire festival of Samhain, with its Pagan rituals, was "Christianized" in 835 AD; November 1st became All Saint's Day, and the previous day, October 31st, Hallowe'en.

Pagan rituals were slow to disappear and although some of the customs became spread around the calendar, the belief persisted that spirits and ghosts came out in force at this time. People were ignorant and very superstitious; they set great store by the old beliefs, and lived in fear of witches and their dark dealings. They believed that at Hallowe'en all evil things were stirred up and ready for mischief. Loud feasting, banging of drums, and huge

fires to light up the night sky would all serve to drive away the Devil and his accomplices. Fairies had been known to spirit away young wives for a year and a day and to snatch babies from their cradles. Werewolves could be heard howling; dead hands seemed to reach out from under gravestones.

Some areas developed their own rituals for the celebration of Hallowe'en. In Perthshire the villagers piled wood and gorse onto a huge Bronze Age barrow in the belief that it contained the remains of plague victims. They set fire to it, and the young lads would take burning brands from the fire and parade round the fields with them, while the village people held hands and danced round the barrow. When the fire had died down the boys leapt backward and forward over the embers. In Northamptonshire everyone met at the church gate at midnight on Hallowe'en to form a tin-can band, to go around the village making as much noise as possible to drive away dangerous spirits.

In Hinton St. George, Somerset, "Punkie Night" was when children made "punkies" from large mangolds given to them by farmers. Making the lanterns, scooping out the flesh of the mangold, cutting little windows, and then getting hold of a piece of candle to go inside was all part of the build-up to the parade round the village; singing, "It's Punkie Night tonight".

The custom was supposed to have originated when long ago some Hinton St. George men went to Chiselborough or Chinnock Fair. They all got drunk and lost their way home, so their wives improvised lanterns and set out to look for them.

Most of the magic spells associated with Hallowe'en were comparatively harmless, consisting of charms and divination to reveal who would be married and when. A sprig of yew from a strange churchyard placed under a girl's pillow would produce a dream of her future husband as would placing her shoes in a "T" shape beside the bed—a very powerful spell this, for the T represented the hammer of the very strong Norse god, Thor. Numerous charms involved the skins of apples, or hazelnuts in the fire, resulting in the future husband's name being spelt out, or his form appearing in a mirror. A well-known charm was for a girl to run three times round the church as the clock struck midnight, sowing hemp seed as she ran. This practice would be illegal today, but until about 200 years ago, hemp was grown in many country districts for making into rope and canvas. The girl sowing the seed would sing as she ran, "Hemp seed I sow, hemp seed I hoe, Hoping my true love will come after me and mow." Looking over her shoulder she would see the form of her true love following her with a scythe.

Most of the spells involved midnight, churchyards, and the burning of fires to keep away the evil beings that stalked this night of magic and potential danger. Children today still like to make pumpkin lanterns, though bonfires are now usually saved for Guy Fawkes Day a few days later. Pictures of witches and their cats, or familiars, adorn classroom walls. In recent years the American custom of Trick or Treat has become more popular. This is based on the idea that if you do not placate the evil spirits with gifts of money or sweets, they will play a nasty trick on you. Children dress up as "ghoulies and ghosties and long-leggety beasties," and go up and down the streets knocking on doors, thus keeping alive one of the ancient Pagan rituals of our ancestors.

The date of Hallowe'en is still a definite turning point in the countryside. As November unfolds, the last few leaves drift off the tired trees; one or two apples still hang on the leafless branches; the afternoon sun has only a little warmth left in its rays. Soon the shortening days will bring a chill to the air, and the dead hand of winter will hold every living thing in its grip. The Earth will sleep through the long, dark winter until that first flower, the Fair Maid of February, the snowdrop, lifts her graceful head above the glistening snow to begin again the cycle of the seasons.

November 18:
The Feast of Baba Yaga

By Edain McCoy

Baba Yaga is the supreme crone Goddess of old Russia, who was once honored with a feast day during the full moon of November. Her once revered image has taken a severe beating in modern times. She is now most often portrayed as a "wicked old witch," complete with nose warts and a hunchback. Russian children are sometimes coerced into behaving themselves through admonitions that if they are not good, Baba Yaga will catch them and cook them for supper.

Honegar: A European Magical Tonic

By Edain McCoy

Honegar, a blend of raw honey and cider vinegar, is a general tonic for health and vigor which is still used throughout Western Europe today. In rural Germany, it can even be bought from the local apothecary. Its origins in history are foggy, but many believe that the brew grew out of a combination of natural medicinal practices and Pagan religious beliefs.

In Europe, honey has long been associated with personal stamina, sexuality, and boosting of the immune system. Cider vinegar and its apple juice prototypes were associated with healing and purification, the apple being sacred to many European goddesses. Modern medical evidence supports the view that vinegar has the ability to wash impurities from the body, particularly from the kidneys and urinary tract.

Drinking as little as a scant quarter cup a day is thought to promote general health and longevity. This recipe should make enough doses for two people for thirty days:

1 1/2 pounds raw honey
32 ounces apple cider vinegar
A large non-metal pan, at least a six-quart size
6 sterilized, standard-sized canning jars or other
    heat resistant containers with snug lids

Place the honey and vinegar into the pan and stir over medium heat. Do not stop stirring, and be sure to get the spoon well into the bottom of the pan to bring up the heavy honey which will settle there. As the mixture warms, the heavy feeling will begin to lighten and you will get the feel of the ingredients blending together.

After about ten minutes (the timing will vary depending upon the calibration of your stove), the Honegar should be blended thoroughly enough to remove from the heat.

Allow the solution to cool for about thirty minutes, giving it a stir every now and then. With a funnel, drain the Honegar into the sterilized containers and seal. It will keep for up to six weeks when refrigerated.

Magical folk usually like to charge and bless their Honegar under a Full Moon or a midday Sun before using. To do this, simply take the jars outdoors, or to an open window, and hold them up where you can feel the light of the Sun/Moon flowing into the solution. Channel the blessings of the heavenly body, and the deities it represents, filling the jars.

Drink a quarter cup of your charged Honegar each day to help sustain good health, youth, and stamina. If you find the taste of the straight Honegar unpleasant, it can be blended into a glass of water or tea.

A Boiling Potpourri for the Magical Kitchen

By Edain McCoy

Before you brew up that next Kitchen Witch's spell, trying setting a boiling potpourri to work first to purify and protect the magical environment of your kitchen. The herbal fragrance of this compound is very appealing, and can probably be made with items you already have on hand. If you don't have all the items, feel free to eliminate or substitute to suit your own needs and tastes. In a medium-sized sauce pan, mix:

    2 cups tap water
    15 cloves
    6 small cinnamon sticks
    8 bruised nutmeg cloves
    1/4 cup dried pumpkin
    1 apple, chopped into 1/4 inch pieces
        (dried apples work best)
    2 tablespoons dried orange peel
    1 tablespoon vanilla extract
    1 teaspoon dried hyssop
    1 dash lemon juice

Allow the potpourri to simmer gently on a back burner of your stove while its magic works for you.

Holiday Baking Tips

By Patricia Telesco

Every civilization has festivals based either on religious obser-
vances or the turning of the seasons. These are joyous days set
aside for fun; a momentary rest from toils, gatherings with
friends and offerings to the gods, and there are almost always
special types of edibles and beverages for everyone to enjoy.
While the antiquated meanings behind many of our holidays
have been lost to time and commercialism, there is no reason
not to reclaim that special atmosphere through food.

Consider for a moment how meaningful those old recipes from your aunt or grandmother are to you and your family. Each time that particular meal is prepared, it carries with it the energy of memories.

Take the example of New Year's Day. This is a time of fresh beginnings for most people, when wishes of joy, health, and happiness are exchanged. One old custom for this day was to have cakes, cheeses, and breads prepared alongside a hot pint of ale for any visitor who happened by after midnight and through the following morning. This tradition was known in Victorian times as "visiting day." Eggnog, candies, and nuts would often adorn a sideboard as a sign of hospitality.

Carrying traditions like this into your home with your own style can give them new meaning. Here are some examples:

St. Patrick's Day: Invoke the luck of the Irish. Prepare any naturally green foods or add a little food coloring. Since the clover is the symbol of good fortune in Ireland, make cookies shaped in that fashion. Consider a main dish of Irish stew with garnishes noted for their fortunate energies. Examples include poppy seed rolls, a fruit salad with strawberries, pineapple and oranges, a cabbage salad, or huckleberry muffins for dessert.

Easter: The name Easter comes from the Teutonic Goddess Ostern (in Scandinavia Ostra and in Anglo Saxon Eastore) whose appearance signals the coming of spring. Ancient forms of this festival celebrate the life of the land, productivity, fertility, and refreshed energy. If you find you need any of these aspects brought into your life, consider traditional egg dishes of any sort. The golden

color of the egg yolk is likened to the Sun, the food itself is an excellent charm for fruitfulness. Hot cross buns are an Anglo Saxon treat from Pagan times. These can be prepared to honor the season and bring renewed balance to your life. The equal-armed cross on the buns represents the four directions and the wheel of time.

Harvest Festivals: Be it Thanksgiving, Halloween, or the local farmers' celebration, harvest festivals mark the end of summer's warmth and a time to be more conservative. They have also been regarded as days to share your bounty with others in need. Harvest times stand in the balance between summer and winter. Halloween is especially appropriate for communication with the spirit world and divining the future. All of these ideas can be worked into your feasts in numerous ways. To improve your psychic insights for divination, serve pomegranate seeds, figs, cherries and oranges in a horn of plenty, or offer a dandelion salad for a side dish. To show your gratitude to the earth, make a pumpkin bread pudding, saving any extra crumbs for the birds and other small animals outdoors. Apple wines or meads can be prepared for health through the coming cold season, and if you pour a little at the bases of your trees it is thought to help bring bounty to them again the next year.

Other Options: Remember that any day of the year, if approached with a special attitude, can be a holiday. All it takes is a little extra thought and imagination to inspire magic in any meal. Consider the season, any dates of personal significance and/or normal calendar celebrations as a starting point. To this add themes of color, scent, flavor, and even decorations to accent the magical meanings behind your dishes. Most of all, enjoy your craftsmanship.

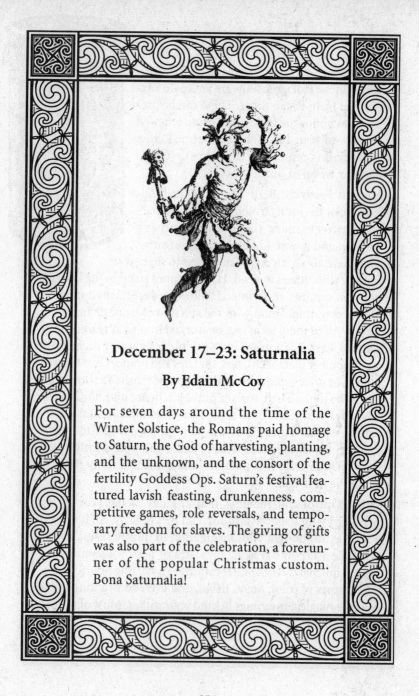

December 17–23: Saturnalia

By Edain McCoy

For seven days around the time of the Winter Solstice, the Romans paid homage to Saturn, the God of harvesting, planting, and the unknown, and the consort of the fertility Goddess Ops. Saturn's festival featured lavish feasting, drunkenness, competitive games, role reversals, and temporary freedom for slaves. The giving of gifts was also part of the celebration, a forerunner of the popular Christmas custom. Bona Saturnalia!

Give the Gift of Magick

By Silver RavenWolf

Yule Ornament

Purpose: To bring prosperity and protection to the home.

Timing: On a Sunday, or during a New Moon, or when the Moon is in Cancer, or during the planetary hour of the Sun.

Supplies:

1 wooden Christmas tree ornament
    shaped like a house
1 dab of honey
Black acrylic paint and 00 number brush
1/2 ounce of mistletoe, steeped in warm water
    (if you can only get dried), or
Three mistletoe berries

Steps:

1. Cleanse and consecrate the ornament.

2. Consecrate the paint and honey. Mix together. Empower for prosperity.

3. Cleanse and consecrate mistletoe. Empower for protection.

4. Paint your house number on the ornament with the paint/honey mixture.

5. Paint pentacles on all the doors and windows.

6. Coat the bottom of the ornament with the mistletoe mixture or crush the three berries on the bottom of the ornament.

7. After it is dry, hold the ornament in both hands and offer it to the heavens. Ground and center.

8. Imagine the little ornament filling with white light of happiness, joy, protection, and wealth.

9. Hold this image until the little house vibrates in your hands. Ground and center.

10. Hang the ornament on your Yule tree.

11. Renew the charm next year.

Gift for a Special Day

Purpose: To provide a working tool. This string of beads can be used as a meditation tool or a tool for petitioning prayers.

Timing: Make over either a Full or New Moon or on a Monday or when the planetary hour is in the Moon or when the Moon is in Aries.

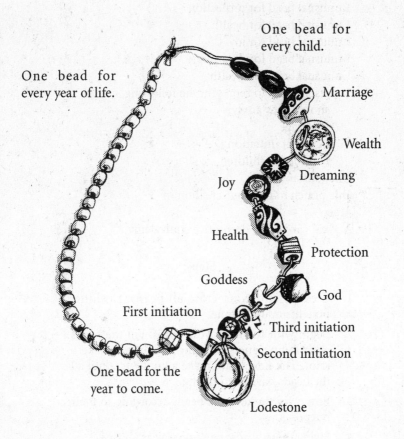

One bead for every child.

One bead for every year of life.

Marriage

Wealth

Dreaming

Joy

Health

Protection

Goddess

God

First initiation

Third initiation

Second initiation

One bead for the year to come.

Lodestone

Supplies:

1 one and a half to two yard long piece of rawhide—
    choose the color carefully
1 bead for every year of life
1 bead for the next year
1 unusual bead to represent the Goddess
1 unusual bead to represent the God
1 unusual bead for protection
1 unusual bead for health
1 unusual bead for joy
1 unusual bead for dreaming
1 unusual bead for wealth
1 unusual bead to represent the following,
    should they apply:
    Marriage
    Levels of initiation
    Number of children
One lodestone
One pouch to put your creation in
A pen
A 3"x5" card or its decorative equivalent

Steps:

1. Cleanse and consecrate all beads, rawhide, pouch, and lodestone.

2. Begin with the birth year beads. Fill the beads with loving energy. String one bead, make a knot. The next bead, make a knot, etc. until all the beads have been strung.

3. Empower the unusual beads according to their purposes.

4. String these beads the same way as above.

5. Empower the lodestone to draw positive energy toward your gift recipient. Attach the lodestone to the end of the string either by tying it on and securing it with glue, or placing it inside a piece of jewelry that can be attached to the string.

6 On your 3"x5" card, explain what the gift is and give a key to the beads.

7. Offer the tool to a guardian deity, perhaps for which your friend has an affinity. Be sure to add this information on the card.

8 Place your gift inside the pouch and give it to your friend.

Sun Box

Purpose: To uplift the spirits and chase away the blues.

Timing: Sunday or when the Moon is in Leo or empower when the planetary hour is in the Sun.

Supplies:

1 small, wooden box
Blue acrylic paint
Yellow acrylic paint
White or silver acrylic paint
03 flat brush for blue paint
01 round brush for white or silver paint
Gold sequins
Craft glue
1 small gold candle that will fit inside the box

Steps:

1. Cleanse and consecrate all materials.
2. Paint the box blue on the outside. Allow to dry.
3. Paint small stars in white/silver on the outside of the box. Allow to dry.
4. Paint the inside of the box yellow. Allow to dry.
5. Open box, brush inside bottom with glue. Sprinkle sequins over the glue, cover entire surface. Let dry.
6. Repeat procedure with inside top of box and inside sides.
7. When the timing is right, empower the box with love, divine energy, success, and wisdom.
8. Dress the gold candle with an oil that is pleasing to your purpose. Put it in the box.
9. Close the box. Do not open it again. Seal the box with a bit of wax.
10. Design a card explaining the purpose of the box. On a day when your friend is feeling blue, they are to open the box, relax and burn the candle.

Fateful Stones: A Brief Look at Mysterious Gems

By Patricia Telesco

- ◎ **Opals:** Opals are said to bring misfortune, especially in marriage. Black opals are believed to open the doors to the spirit world.

- ◎ **Diamonds:** Hindus regard flawed diamonds to be especially bad luck. The Hope Diamond was captured in India in the 17th century from a statue of Rama Sita. Since that time it has brought disaster and death to each of its owners.

- ◎ **Onyx:** Considered an ominous stone in Arabic traditions, named the stone of sadness. If worn, it is said to bring doubt, apprehension, nightmares, and contention between friends.

- ◎ **Ruby:** The ruby is supposed to be so aligned with the element of fire that it can not be held in any cloth container.

- ◎ **Green Garnets:** If a person is attracted to these stones, he or she is thought to have a jealous nature.

- ◎ **Agate:** Gives its bearer wanderlust.

- ◎ **Pearl:** In China, pearls are thought to bring sadness, sickness, and fear.

- ◎ **Tiger's Eye:** If exchanged by lovers may cause divorce.

And to You Your Wassail, too!

By Edain McCoy

The Anglo-Celtic custom of wassailing has its roots in ancient folk beliefs about the power in the turning of the seasons, and of baneful spirits and magical healing. On Samhain Eve small communities took weapons, drums, musical instruments, and wassail punch into the forests on a pilgrimage to the various apple trees. The apple was a symbol of the Goddess, and of the hope for eternal rebirth, and therefore had to be protected on this magical night when the season slipped from summer to winter.

Once at the tree, the drums and weapons were noisily discharged to frighten away any ill-meaning spirits dwelling in the boughs. Then the music was played joyously as toasts were offered to the sacred trees with the wassail punch. A central feature of these toasts were pleas for good health in the coming year.

In the Middle Ages, the drink found its way into Christmas celebrations, with many yearly toasts still being offered over the raised mug—minus the trek to the local apple trees and the accompanying noise, of course.

Wassail Punch

2 cups apple juice
1/2 cup heavy cream
1 quart ale (room
    temperature)
1 cup cooking sherry (room temperature)
6 large or 8 medium baked apples, cut into
    bite-sized pieces
5 egg whites
1 1/4 cups granulated sugar
2 teaspoons allspice
1 teaspoon cinnamon
1/2 teaspoon nutmeg
1/2 teaspoon ginger
8 whole cloves
1 large punch bowl

Bring the apple juice, cooked apple bits, and cream to a slow boil, then remove from heat. Beat the egg whites until they are well-beaten, but not frothy. Add the egg whites, and all other ingredients except the alcohol to the juice and cream mix. Blend this together slowly over medium heat until well-mixed. Do not allow it to come to a boil. Allow the mixture to cool just enough so that its heat will not crack your glass punch bowl. Blend in the alcohol and serve. Wassail is always served warm. *Note:* to avoid the possiblity of contracting salmonella from under-cooked egg whites, consider purchasing pasteurized egg whites, which can be found at some grocery stores.

The Yule Wish Tree

By Silver RavenWolf

Often, the items we truly need cannot ride home with us in a bag from the mall during the holiday season countdown. The day before Thanksgiving, take a trip to the tree nursery and find a small, potted evergreen. On your way home, purchase a few yards of red, green, and white ribbon. During the Thanksgiving supper, introduce the tree to the family and the tribe to the tree. Each member of your clan should tie a ribbon on the tree to represent an intangible blessing they would like for the upcoming Yule season. Wishes could be for peace, enough rest, health, etc. Bless the tree and set it where it will have enough light.

When family and friends visit, explain the purpose of the wish tree to them and give them a ribbon to tie on the tree, too. The tree is for everyone. If you plan to use the tree in ritual, have everyone participating make a small ornament, empowered for strengths like self-esteem, goal planning, security, etc. and hang it on the tree while connecting with the divinity of their choice.

On the first day of February, remove all the ornaments and ribbons. Burn the ribbons and cast the ashes to the winds. Pack the ornaments away. Next year, when you open the box, you can de-magick the ornaments and return them to their owners, or hang them on your big tree in memory of last year's prosperity. Continue to take good care of the tree over the remaining winter months. Don't forget to give it water and plenty of love. In the spring, you can plant the tree outside on your property or on the property of a friend.

The Twelve Days of Christmas

By Mary Brown

Our best-loved Christian festival has origins which are deeply rooted in pagan practice. The invading Romans introduced the idea of a twelve-day Midwinter feast, decorating their homes with evergreen branches and giving themselves over to riotous enjoyment. The focus of these festivities was the birthday of the great Sun god, Sol Invictus, or the "Unconquerable Sun" at the winter solstice. This winter "Saturnalia" was not dedicated to the birth of Christ until the fourth century.

Later, when the Norsemen crossed the North Sea, first to pillage and then to settle, they brought the legends about the mistletoe and the Yule log, and the tales of Woden who rode across the sky in his chariot, bearing gifts. For country folk, until comparatively recent times, the bringing in of the Yule log was an important part of the celebration. It was often so large that it took six men to carry it in on Christmas Eve. In the West Country it was sometimes called a "back-brand;" and in some areas it took the form of a bundle of ash sticks bound together into a log. This would be the subject of some harmless divination rites, with young girls trying to guess which band would burst first in the fire, thus showing which of them would marry first. For maximum good fortune the Yule log had to be kept burning for the whole twelve-day period. Afterward a small piece of the ember was kept to light next year's fire; this was believed to serve as fire protection for the household throughout the coming year.

Christmas decorations were put up on Christmas Eve, too, never before. Evergreens were revered as sacred trees long before the birth of Christ, for in these trees the wood spirits dwelt when all the other trees had lost their leaves. Holly was particularly good for protecting against evil spirits and mistletoe has always been good for kissing under. This custom has ancient Celtic origins, having descended from a fertility rite.

Mince pies were already popular in the 16th century, as were plum pudding and plum porridge, which was like a thick soup with meats and fruits boiled together. The first mince pies contained meat as well as fruit, and ideally, one should be eaten in each of twelve different houses over the twelve days.

Turkeys were introduced from the New World in the 16th century, but goose had been the traditional favorite for Christmas dinner until then, and continued to be so for English country folk until the 1940s. The boar's head, so prominent in representations of medieval feasting, was a sacred dish which had originally graced the table of the old Norse gods.

Our Santa Claus is a direct descendant of Saint Nicholas, who is celebrated mainly in Holland and Germany on the 6th of December. The legends of St. Nicholas grew up during early Christian times and took over those of the pagan god Woden.

Boxing Day comes from the old custom of servants and workers taking round collecting boxes to their employers in the hope of receiving gifts. On the last day of December, New Year's Eve, household fires were kept in all night. Fire festivals are still a prominent feature in many parts of Great Britain around this time of year. The old year draws to its close in a climax of feasting. The nights are long but they will soon begin to shorten. Such customs are clearly descended from the old sun-worshipping rituals practiced by our ancestors.

The new year starts mid-way through the twelve days—the month January getting its name from the Roman god Janus, the god of entrances and doorways. He is always depicted with two faces, one to look back at the old year, and one looking forward to the future.

Most people know that the Christmas decorations should come down on Twelfth Night, and that back luck will follow if this is not done. Only one sprig of holly was allowed to remain, hanging in the cowshed to bring good fortune to the cattle. Traditionally the Christmas celebrations came to an end on this day, and from early times, Twelfth Night saw the most riotous parties of all. It was also time for the old West Country custom of wassailing, a survival of a fertility rite in which the apple trees, once the mainstay of the local economy, were given a party with noise, fires, and feasting. Copious amounts of the local cider were consumed and poured upon the ground as a kind of blessing. The ceremony survives at Carnampton in Somerset.

Twelfth Night is also the Christian festival Epiphany—the day of the Three Kings and "Old Christmas Day," so called because when changes were made to the calendar in 1752, eleven days were lopped from the year to correct inaccuracies that had crept into the calendar. This was also the day when the Holy Thorn at Glastonbury was said to flower. The legend tells how Joseph of Arimathea arrived at Glastonbury, Somerset, by boat in 67 AD. He planted his staff in the ground on Wearyall Hill, and it immediately burst into leaf and blossom. Glastonbury was the focus of Christian pilgrimage for many centuries.

After the festivities of Twelfth Night, the pattern of country life resumed its old routine with Plough Monday, on the following Monday. The ploughs were taken out of the barns and blessed. The next festival of significance would be Shrove Tuesday in February or early March. Till then, there was the ploughing to be done, and a good many dark evenings before the returning sun would begin to warm the frozen earth and coax the spring flowers into new life.

Directory
of Products
and Services

Abbe Bassett
Personal Astrology Services

Vocational Guidance: Explores your birthchart to reveal your potential. Very effective for those beginning work, making career changes, or stuck in dead end jobs. Describe what you enjoy, your talents, training, and job experience. $50

Complete Natal Report: Discusses your birth chart in response to your specific concerns and provides insights to their resolution. Defines your transits and progressions and solar arc directions for one year and introduces spiritual lessons contained in them. $85

Compatibility: This is a useful tool for discovering the relationship dynamics between you and a lover, partner, friend, or enemy. Send birth data for both people. $65

Child Guidance: Provides a useful tool in discovering the emerging personality of your child. Shows how your child relates to you, his or her environment, school, and friends. Illuminates interests and talents. $65

Solar Return: Gives a clear picture of what to expect in the coming birthday year. Deals with trends and influences for the year as well as personal dynamics and what the year will bring. $65

Horary: Cast for the moment of an inquiry, reveals issues related to the question and trends pertaining to the matters involved. Deals with influences concerned with the resolution of the question. $65.

Detailed Natal: Deals with a specific set of questions in view of transiting influences, solar arc directions and progressions for the year. Provides answers which are specific in nature. $65.

Speculation Reading: Provides lucky numbers and dates based on your horoscope and name. (Please give full name!) Discusses lucky trends, influences and investments in your life. Gives an outline of luck in your life. $65.

Send a detailed letter with your birth data: month, day, year, time of day, city, state, country where you were born, with check to:

Abbe Bassett
Personal Astrology Services
P.O. Box 17, Essex Junction VT 05453-3030
Please allow 3-5 weeks for your order to be completed.

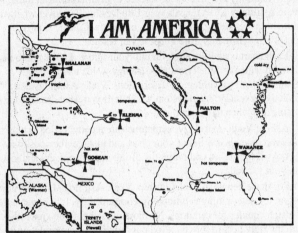

The Stardust Seminary

Craft of the Wise
Correspondence Course

★ *The Stardust Circle is an active Wiccan community with a regular schedule of Sabbats, Esbats, and other events.*

★ *Now you can join us at home to study Witchcraft with our special correspondence course.*

★ *The course is divided into five affordable units of six lessons each on cassette tape.*

★ *Both the Circle and the Seminary are "open". We invite you to visit us!*

To begin your adventure in Wicca, send a check or money order for just $25 for the first unit, *An Introduction to Wicca*, to:

The Stardust Circle
Seminary Admissions Office
PO Box 2474, Durham, NC 27715

Or send a long, self addressed, stamped envelope for more information.

PSYCHIC LINE

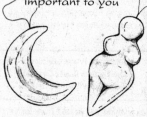

Classifieds

Products

UNIQUE DESIGNS "BORN Again Pagan" or "Howl at the Moon" - button $1.50, bumper sticker $2. 8" diameter iron-on transfer $5. Catalog $1., free w/order. KLW Enterprises, 3790 El Camino Real, #270A, Palo Alto CA 94306-3314

Publications

THE CRYSTAL MOON, International Metaphysical Digest. From The Order of the Crystal Moon, International Fellowship. Quarterly, 8 ½ x 11, 70+ pages, in envelope. WPPA member press. International writers: Wicca, Huna, Goddess Spirituality, herbs, networking , more. Fellowship of Isis and Wiccan Correspondence courses. Sample /information U.S. $6.50. Astrology/Occult Catalog U.S. $3., refundable. Box 802-MA, Matteson IL 60443-0802

Readings

EXTRAORDINARY PSYCHIC COUNSELOR, Randal Clayton Bradford, will tell you the best possible future in any situation, and how to make it happen. "Cuts straight to the truth"…accurate, detailed and specific." Established worldwide clientele by telephone. AMEX/MC/Visa 310-823-8893 or 213-REALITY

CLARIFY YOUR LIFE! Anna Victor Hale—Psychic-Astro-Intuitive counseling. $1.99 per min. MC/VISA/M.O., 800-438-1266

ACCURATE TELEPHONE READINGS by experienced clairvoyant counselor. By appointment. Susan 301-645-1226

PSYCHIC SPIRITUALIST REUNITES all lost loves. Lamarr Dell, a natural-born gifted psychic, has abilities to restore love, happiness, business, health. One phone reading will give you peace of mind. 900-287-7924 or 818 760-8424 $2.49/min.

PSYCHIC PHONE READINGS, incredibly accurate. Need answers on love, health, finances? JoAnna, 516-753-0191, $35.

KNOW THYSELF. SIMULACRA of your soul. For free information write to: P.O. Box 776, Mesilla Park NM 88047

LIVE READINGS! 90% ACCURATE psychic astrological answers. Walk through other's minds! $2.40 per minute. Checks by phone, Mastercard/VISA 800-488-3786

JOIN OUR PSYCHIC Calling Card™ family for the reading of your lifetime. Live! 24 hours. 1-800-549-7337 or 1-900-773-7374 ext. 5625. $3.99/min. 18+. Neat Stuff Catalogue.$2. The Psychic Network® Box 499-MA, Deerfield FL 33443

Reincarnation

THE TWO CRUCIFIXIONS Poster-size illustration of the star figures and configuration of the heavens which was the first Bible and the common ancestor of almost all religion. Included is a booklet of explanation. $15. 675 Fairview Drive, #246, Carson City NV 89701

Llewellyn's Computerized Astrological Services

Llewellyn has been a leading authority in astrological chart readings for over thirty years. Our professional experience and continued dedication assures complete satisfaction in all areas of our astrological services.

Llewellyn features a wide variety of readings with the intent to satisfy the needs of any astrological enthusiast. Our goal is to give you the best possible service so that you can achieve your goals and live your life successfully.

When requesting a computerized service be sure to give accurate and complete birth data including: exact time (a.m. or p.m.), date, year, city, county and country of birth. (Check your birth certificate for this information.) *Accuracy of birth data is very important.* Llewellyn will not be responsible for mistakes made by you. An order form follows for your convenience.

Computerized Charts

Simple Natal Chart

Before you do anything else, order the Simple Natal Chart! This chart print-out is programmed and designed by Matrix. Learn the locations of your midpoints and aspects, elements, and more. Discover your planets and house cusps, retrogrades and other valuable data necessary to make a complete interpretation.

APS03-119 . . . . $5.00

Transit Report

Know the trends of your life—in advance! Keep abreast of positive trends and challenging periods for a specified period of time in your life. Transits are the relationships between the planets today and their positions at the moment of your birth. They are an invaluable aid for timing your actions and making decisions. This report devotes a paragraph to each of your transit aspects and gives effective dates for those transits. The report will begin with the first day of the month. Be sure to specify present residence for all people getting this report!

APS03-500 – 3-month report $12.00
APS03-501 – 6-month report $20.00
APS03-502 – 1-year report $30.00

Personality Profile

This is our most popular reading! It makes the perfect gift! This ten-part reading gives you a complete look at your "natal imprint" and how the planets mark your destiny. Examine your emotional needs and inner feelings. Explore your imagination and read about your general characteristics and life patterns. Very reasonable price!

APS03-503 . . . . $20.00

Life Progression

Discover what the future has in store for you! This incredible reading covers a year's time and is designed to complement the Personality Profile Reading. Progressions are a special system with which astrologers map how the "natal you" develops through specified periods of your present and future life. We are all born into an already existing world and an already existing fabric of personal interaction, and with this report you can discover the "now you!"

APS03-507 . . . .$20.00

Personal Relationship Interpretation

If you've just called it quits on one relationship and know you need to understand more about yourself before you test the waters again, then this is the report for you! This reading will tell you how you approach relationships in general, what kind of people you look for and what kind of people might rub you the wrong way. Important for anyone!

APS03-506 . . . . $20.00

Tarot Reading

Find out what the cards have in store for you with this 12-page report that features a ten-card "Celtic Cross" spread. This reading is custom made to answer any question you specify. For every card that turns up there is a detailed corresponding explanation of what each means for you. Order this tarot reading today!

APS03-120 . . . . $10.00

Lucky Lotto Report (State Lottery Report)

Do you play the state lotteries? This report will determine your luckiest sequence of numbers for each day based on specific planets, degrees and other indicators in your own chart. Provide your full birth data and middle name, and specify the parameters of your state's lottery: i.e., how many numbers you need in sequence (up to 10 numbers) as well as the highest possible numeral (up to #999). Indicate the month you want to start.

APS03-512 – 3-month report $10.00
APS03-513 – 6-month report $15.00
APS03-514 – 1-year report $25.00

Numerology Report

Find out which numbers are right for you with this insightful report. This report uses an ancient form of numerology invented by Pythagoras to determine the significant numbers in your life. Using both your given birth name and date of birth, this report will accurately calculate those numbers which stand out as yours. With these numbers, the report can determine certain trends in your life and tell you when the important periods of your life will occur.

APS03-508 – 3-month report $12.00
APS03-509 – 6-month report $18.00
APS03-510 – 1-year report $25.00

Compatibility Profile

Find out if you really are compatible with your lover, spouse, friend or business partner! This is a great way of getting an in-depth look at your relationship with another person. Find out each person's approach to the relationship. Do you have the same goals? How well do you deal with arguments? Do you have the same values? This service includes planetary placements for both individuals, so send birth data for both. Succeed in all of your relationships! Order today!

APS03-504 . . . . $30.00

Biorhythm Report

Ever have one of those days when you have unlimited energy and everything is going your way? Then the next day you are feeling sluggish and awkward? These cycles are called biorhythms. This individual report will accurately map your daily biorhythms. It can be your personal guide to the cycles of your daily life. Each important day is thoroughly discussed. With this valuable information, you can schedule important events with great success. This report is an invaluable source of information to help you plan your days to the fullest. Order today!

APS03-515 – 3-month report $12.00
APS03-516 – 6-month report $18.00
APS03-517 – 1-year report $25.00

Ultimate Astro-Profile

This report has it all! Receive over 40 pages of fascinating, insightful and uncanny descriptions of your innermost qualities and talents. Read about your burn rate (thirst for change). Explore your personal patterns (inside and outside). Examine the particular pattern of your Houses. The Astro-Profile doesn't repeat what you've already learned from other personality profiles, but considers often the neglected natal influence of the lunar nodes plus much more.

APS03-505 . . . . $40.00

SPECIAL COMBO OFFER

Personality Profile & Life Progression

Know yourself and know your future! This powerful
combination of readings can help you understand
what challenges lie ahead and what resources you
have to achieve the success you want.

Special Combo Price!
APS03-216 $30.00

Astrological Services Order Form

Remember to include all birth data plus your full name for all reports.
Receive a 25% discount on any <u>one</u> additional computer
report when you order the SIMPLE NATAL CHART.

Service name and number _____

Full name (1st person) _____

Birthtime_____ ❐ a.m. ❐ p.m.   Date _____ Year _____

Birthplace (city, county, state, country) _____

_____

Full name (2nd person) _____

Birthtime_____ ❐ a.m. ❐ p.m.   Date _____ Year _____

Birthplace (city, county, state, country) _____

_____

Name _____

Address _____

City _____ State _____ Zip _____

Make check or money order payable to Llewellyn Publications, or charge it!

❐ VISA   ❐ MasterCard   ❐ American Express

Account Number _____ Expiration Date _____

Day Phone _____ Signature _____

Mail this form and payment to: Llewellyn's Personal Services,
P.O. Box 64383-K906, St. Paul MN 55164-0383. *Allow 4-6 weeks for delivery.*

The Astrologer's Datebook

Astrologers everywhere make the *Daily Planetary Guide* an integral part of their lives each year because it's brimming with the day-to-day planetary information they need: all the major daily planetary aspects and motions including retrogrades, directs and sign changes; aspects for the four major asteroids and Chiron; the Moon's sign, phase, and voids-of-course; and exact times for all listed in both Eastern and Pacific time.

Also featured are old favorites "A Stargazer's Guide to Celestial Phenomena," a monthly ephemeris, sunrise and sunset tables and plenty of space to jot down appointments and reminders.

Nationally known astrologer Tom Jerome Roma returns with another year of detailed weekly forecasts to help you pinpoint how the planets will affect your life in 1995.

- **Look up daily aspects quickly and easily**

- **Better understand yourself in the context of "the astrological calendar" with the weekly forecasts**

- **Track the visibility of the planets with the 1995 guide to celestial phenomena**

- **Consult the directory of professional astrologers from around the world**

Llewellyn's 1995 Daily Planetary Guide
288 pp. ✦ wire-o-binding ✦ 5 ¼ x 8 ✦ Order # K-900 ✦ $7.95

Please use order form on last page.

SUPER DISCOUNTS ON
LLEWELLYN DATEBOOKS AND CALENDARS!

Llewellyn offers several ways to save money on our almanacs and calendars. With a four-year subscription you receive your books as soon as they are published. The price remains the same for four years even if there is a price increase! Llewellyn pays postage and handling. *Buy any 2 subscriptions and take $2 off! Buy 3 and take $3 off! Buy 4 and take an additional $5 off the cost!*

Subscriptions (4 years, 1996-1999)

❑	Astrological Calendar	$40.00
❑	Sun Sign Book	$19.96
❑	Moon Sign Book	$19.96
❑	Daily Planetary Guide	$31.80
❑	Organic Gardening Almanac	$23.80

Order *by the dozen* and save 40%! Sell them to your friends or give them as gifts. Llewellyn pays all postage and handling on quantity orders.

Quantity Orders: 40% OFF

1995	1996		
❑	❑	Astrological Calendar	$72.00
❑	❑	Sun Sign Book	$35.93
❑	❑	Moon Sign Book	$35.93
❑	❑	Daily Planetary Guide	$57.24
❑	❑	Magical Almanac	$50.04
❑	❑	Organic Gardening Almanac	$42.84
❑	❑	Myth and Magic Calendar	$72.00

When ordering individual copies, include $3 postage for orders under $10 and $4 for orders over $10. Llewellyn pays postage for all orders over $50.

Individual copies of Llewellyn Almanacs and Calendars

1995	1996		
❑	❑	Astrological Calendar	$10.00
❑	❑	Sun Sign Book	$4.99
❑	❑	Moon Sign Book	$4.99
❑	❑	Daily Planetary Guide	$7.95
❑	❑	Magical Almanac	$6.95
❑	❑	Organic Gardening Almanac	$5.95
❑	❑	Myth and Magic Calendar	$10.00

Please use order form on last page.

LLEWELLYN ORDER FORM

Llewellyn Publications
P.O. Box 64383-K906, St. Paul, MN 55164-0383

You may use this form to order any of the Llewellyn books or services listed in this publication.

Give Title, Author, Order Number and Price.

_____

_____

_____

_____

_____

Shipping and Handling: We ship UPS when possible. Include $3 for orders $10 and under and $4 for orders over $10. Llewellyn pays postage for all orders over $50. Please give street address (UPS cannot deliver to P.O. Boxes).
Next Day Air cost—$16.00/one book; add $2.00 for each additional book.
Second Day Air cost—$7.00/one book; add $1.00 for each additional book.

Credit Card Orders: In the U.S. and Canada call 1-800-THE-MOON. In Minnesota call 612-291-1970. Or, send credit card order by mail. Any questions can be directed to customer service 612-291-1970.

❏ Yes! Send me your free catalog!

❏ VISA   ❏ MasterCard   ❏ American Express

Account No. _____

Expiration Date _____ Phone _____

Signature _____

Name _____

Address _____

City _____ State _____ Zip _____

Thank you for your order!